The Family Portrait

—————— SECOND EDITION ——————

A Compilation of Data, Research
and Public Opinion on the Family

Bridget Maher, Editor

FAMILY RESEARCH COUNCIL

The Family Portrait: A Compilation of Data,
Research and Public Opinion on the Family
Second Edition
ISBN 1-55872-011-1
©2004 by the Family Research Council
All rights reserved.

Family Research Council
801 G Street, N.W.
Washington, DC 20001

Printed in the United States of America
Art Direction and Design by Kimberly Manning

CONTENTS

ACKNOWLEDGEMENTS

I would like to express special thanks to Nancy Unsworth,
Maggie Niehaus, Allan Carlson and Kimberly Manning.

I would also like to acknowledge the assistance of Witherspoon Fellows
Jessica Hooten, Erica Little, Christine Howe and Emily Brown.

INTRODUCTION

Allan Carlson and Bill Saunders

The United Nations has designated 2004 as the International Year of the Family. Technically, it is the "10th Anniversary" of the year originally chosen by the United Nations to be the first "Year of the Family" (1994), but the significant point is that the nations of the world have chosen this year to focus on the family.

Such a focus is appropriate. The family has always been recognized, across cultures, as fundamental to a healthy society. In the modern era, the world community has acknowledged the importance of the family in its foundational human rights document, the Universal Declaration of Human Rights. Article 16 declares: "Men and women of full age, without any limitation due to race, nationality or religion, have the right to marry and to found a family." Section 3 of Article 16 goes on to state: "The family is the natural and fundamental group unit of society and is entitled to protection by society and the State." Article 16 thus expresses the universal consensus regarding the importance of the natural family as well as the obligation of the government to respect it.

There will be many meetings around the world during 2004 to reflect upon the importance of the family. Family Research Council is pleased to help facilitate a series of meetings, the "Intercultural Dialogue on the Family," which will convene in Mexico City, Stockholm, Venice, Qatar and Manila. Through these meetings, organizations around the world that are concerned with the state of the natural family and its fundamental role in society will have an opportunity to identify and examine problems and to reflect jointly on policies that might resolve them.

The 2004 edition of *The Family Portrait* comes at an auspicious time, providing information that should help policy makers not only in the United States but around the world by supplying data by which to evaluate the health of the family. Although the majority of the data in *The Family Portrait* is from the United States, we feel it will prove helpful to other nations as well. Trends in the United States are to some extent representative of those in the Western industrial (or post-industrial, informational) world. Thus, if other nations develop similarly, data from the United States may provide an indication of trends they may expect to see in their own nations.

Public policy has always had a strong role in both tracking and determining these trends. In the early 1930s, the Swedish economist Gunnar Myrdal penned an influential article on "The Dilemma of Social Policy." A socialist, he argued that new research techniques in social science had transformed the disciplines of sociology and psychology into radical tools. Public policy in the past, he continued, had aimed at relieving symptoms of social disorder, and so gave help to the sick, the poor, and the unemployed. In practice, Myrdal said, such an approach merely reinforced traditional ways of doing things. However, new tools of analysis now allowed policymakers to aim at *preventive* social policy, which would forestall social pathologies. When based on humane value premises and rational science, this *preventive* social policy led to "the natural marriage" of the correct technical and the politically radical solution.

For the middle decades of the Twentieth Century, until about 1980, this was the general assumption: social science was the friend of left-liberal policy innovation. Traditional institutions, the argument went, rested on irrational arrangements, prejudice, and exploitation, all of which a reason-guided social science would expose. Indeed, the more energetic voices claimed the ability to become social engineers, crafting a wholly new social order, and even a new human type. By the 1970s, the field of sociology became almost synonymous with radical politics.

In recent decades, though, deeper truths have re-emerged. As Robert Nisbet reminds us, the discipline of sociology actually developed during the late 19th Century among conservatives such as Emile Durkheim, who pondered the dramatic effects of the industrial revolution on traditional life. Honestly done, social science actually probes into and reveals the immutable realities of human nature. Rather than opening human life up to reengineering, social science is more apt to expose the folly of such efforts. Social research also illuminates the strengths, indeed the irreplaceability of the traditional family.

This new edition of *The Family Portrait*, edited by Bridget Maher, is a compelling affirmation of the family as the natural and fundamental unit of society. The editor carefully translates complex social science findings into concise, readable, and usable summaries. She shows, for example, that married people are healthier, happier, and longer lived; that married couples reap greater financial rewards; and that women are physically safer in marriage than in any other setting. The editor exposes the failed promises and dismal consequences of cohabitation. Concerning children, Bridget Maher musters the research results showing that they are safest and healthiest in homes with their two natural parents and that they fare better economically and educationally in such settings. She also summarizes the evidence on the negative effects of divorce on children and young adults and the heavy costs imposed on society by single-parenting.

The Family Portrait is much more, though. This volume offers a unique look at current American attitudes toward marriage, families, and children. Some of the news is encouraging. Americans remain committed to the ideal of marriage; they still think that the full-time care of small children by their mothers is best; and they think it's best for a child to be raised by married parents. At the same time, the behavior of many Americans falls well short of their claimed ideals. *The Family Portrait* reports a steady decline in the marriage rate since 1970; a parallel fall in the marital birthrate; a surge in cohabitation; and a dramatic increase in the number of out-of-wedlock births. The book also hints at some of the reasons for this inconsistency: economic stress; the pressure on young mothers to work; the weakness of existing divorce laws; and public policies that fail to protect the family.

A new feature in this edition of *The Family Portrait* is a section on international figures and findings regarding the family. Around the world, men and women are marrying at later ages and marriage rates and fertility rates have significantly declined. Meanwhile divorce, cohabitation and the number of children born out of wedlock have dramatically increased over the past four decades.

Indeed, we commend Bridget Maher's *The Family Portrait* as a valuable tool for all legislators, policy advocates, journalists, researchers, clergy, and citizens concerned with the state of our most important social institution. This book does not claim to give all the answers. Yet it does provide the basic facts and the arguments needed to defend the family from the new, even unprecedented, challenges of the early 21ˢᵗ Century.

Allan Carlson, Ph.D.
Distinguished Fellow in Family Policy Studies, Family Research Council and President of The Howard Center

William L. Saunders, Jr.
Senior Fellow and Human Rights Counsel, Family Research Council

CHAPTER 1

Marriage

Marriage is a fundamental social institution. It is central to the nurture and raising of children. It is the "social glue" that reliably attaches fathers to children. It contributes to the physical, emotional, and economic health of men, women and children, and thus to the nation as a whole. It is also one of the most highly prized of all human relationships and a central life goal of most Americans.

—David Popenoe and
Barbara Dafoe Whitehead
The State of Our Unions 2003

BY THE NUMBERS: THE STATE OF MARRIAGE

SNAPSHOT 1
The marriage rate has dropped by 50 percent since 1950.

- In 2001, the marriage rate in the U.S. was the lowest it has ever been, with only 45.6 marriages per thousand unmarried women.

Marriage Rate for Women Age 15 and Older, Historical

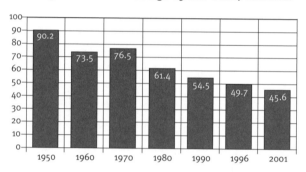

Note: Marriage rate is the annual number of marriages per 1,000 unmarried women age 15 and older.
Source: National Center for Health Statistics [1]

To dare to pledge our whole selves to a single love is the most remarkable thing most of us will ever do.

—Maggie Gallagher
The Abolition of Marriage

SNAPSHOT 2
The percentage of adults who have never married has increased since 1960.

- In 2002, 25.2 percent of women age 15 and older had never married, compared to 19 percent in 1960.

- In 2002, 32 percent of males age 15 and older had never married, compared to 25.3 percent in 1960.

Marital Status of Men and Women Age 15 and Older, Historical

Year	Percent Married		Percent Never Married	
	Men	Women	Men	Women
1950	67.5%	65.8%	26.4%	20.0%
1960	69.3%	65.9%	25.3%	19.0%
1970	66.8%	61.9%	28.1%	22.1%
1980	63.2%	58.9%	29.6%	22.5%
1990	60.7%	56.9%	29.9%	22.8%
1994	59.0%	55.9%	31.2%	23.7%
1996	58.5%	55.6%	31.1%	24.1%
2000	57.9%	54.7%	31.3%	25.1%
2002	57.4%	54.2%	32.0%	25.2%

*1950 and 1960 data are for the population age 14 and older.
Source: U.S. Census Bureau [2]

SNAPSHOT 3
Men and women are marrying at later ages.

- In 2002, the median age at first marriage was 26.9 for men, compared to 23.2 in 1970. For women, it was 25.3 in 2002, compared to 20.8 in 1970.

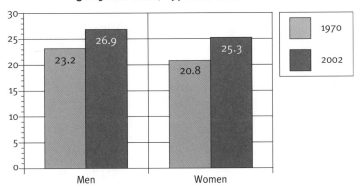

Median Age at First Marriage for Men and Women Age 15 and Older, 1970 and 2002

Median Age at First Marriage for Men and Women Age 15 and Older, Historical

YEAR	MEN'S MEDIAN AGE AT FIRST MARRIAGE	WOMEN'S MEDIAN AGE AT FIRST MARRIAGE
1890	26.1	22.0
1900	25.9	21.9
1910	25.1	21.6
1920	24.6	21.2
1930	24.3	21.3
1940	24.3	21.5
1950	22.8	20.3
1960	22.8	20.3
1970	23.2	20.8
1980	24.7	22.0
1990	26.1	23.9
1994	26.7	24.5
1996	27.1	24.8
1998	26.7	25.0
2000	26.8	25.1
2002	26.9	25.3

Source:
U.S. Census Bureau [3]

SNAPSHOT 4

The percentage of 20- to 34-year-olds who have never married has dramatically increased since 1970.

- From 1970 to 2002, the percentage of never-married men and women age 30-34 more than tripled.

- In 2000, 39 percent of men age 25-34 had never married, compared to 16 percent in 1970.[4]

- In 2000, 30 percent of women age 25-34 had never married, compared to 10 percent in 1970.[5]

Percentage of Never-Married Men and Women Age 20-34, 1970 and 2002

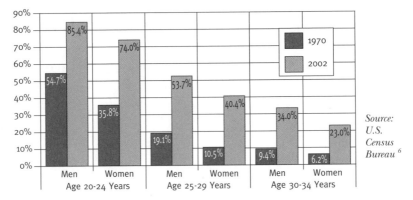

Source: U.S. Census Bureau [6]

THE BENEFITS OF MARRIAGE

SNAPSHOT 1
Married people are happier, healthier and live longer.

- A 1998 study of data from 17 nations found that married men and women report significantly higher levels of happiness than do unmarried people.[7]

- A five-year study released in 1998 found that continuously married people experience better emotional health and less depression than do never-married, remarried, divorced or widowed individuals. The study also reported that getting married for the first time significantly increases a person's emotional well-being.[8]

- A 2003 study of 2,921 mothers found that single mothers were more than twice as likely as married mothers to report an episode of depression during the prior year. Also, compared to married mothers, single mothers report higher levels of stress, fewer contacts with family and friends, less involvement in church or social groups and less social support.[9]

- Data from the National Survey of Family and Households indicates that married people report less depression and fewer alcohol problems than do never-married, separated, divorced or widowed persons. Individuals who marry for the first time or remarry experience a significant decrease in depression, while those who separate or divorce become more depressed.[10]

Decades of social-science research have confirmed the deepest intuitions of the human heart: As frightening, exhilarating, and improbable as this wild vow of constancy may seem, there is no substitute. When love seeks permanence, a safe home for children who long for both parents, when men and women look for someone they can count on, there are no substitutes. The word for what we want is marriage.

—Linda Waite and Maggie Gallagher
*The Case for Marriage: Why Married
People Are Happier, Healthier and Better
Off Financially*

- A 2003 study of young people age 18-35 found that married persons are much less likely to suffer from depression than are single or cohabiting people and that getting married for the first time significantly reduces depression. Those who marry without first cohabiting experience the greatest decrease in depression. According to the study, the fact that marriage reduces depression "emanate[s] from the relationship itself, rather than from the selection of less depressed persons into marriage."[11]

- A 1999 study of 10,005 adults found that those who marry experience a decrease in symptoms of depression, while those who separate from or divorce their spouses experience an increase in depression. The study also found that the positive effects of marriage are greater when individuals believe in the importance of marriage, leading researchers to conclude that people whose behavior is consistent with their beliefs experience better mental health.[12]

- Nationally representative data from the Health and Retirement Survey indicates that, compared to the cohabiting, never-married, divorced and widowed, married persons have the lowest incidences of major diseases and impairments (such as hypertension, diabetes, stroke, heart disease, psychiatric problems, arthritis, back, foot and leg problems). They are also the least likely to be disabled.[13]

- A 1998 study comparing married and widowed elderly persons found that married men and women are much more likely to follow healthy practices, such as exercising, eating breakfast, using seat belts and abstaining from smoking. For example, compared to widowed men, married men are 70 percent more likely to engage in physical activity and twice as likely not to smoke.[14]

- A 2000 national study found that divorced and separated men and women are more than twice as likely as married persons to commit suicide. Divorced men are nearly two-and-a-half times more likely to die from suicide than are married men.[15]

- A 2003 Danish study determined that cohabiting and single people were at higher risk for suicide than were married people.[16]

SNAPSHOT 2
Married couples enjoy greater sexual satisfaction.

The reality seems to be that the quality of the sex is higher and the skill in achieving satisfaction and pleasure is greater when one's limited capacity to please is focused on one partner in the context of a monogamous, long-term partnership.

—Robert T. Michael
The Social Organization of Sexuality: Sexual Practices in the United States

- Of all sexually active people, married couples who are sexually faithful to one another experience the most physical pleasure and emotional satisfaction with their sex lives.[17]

- Faithfully married people reported the most positive feelings about sex; they felt "satisfied," "loved," "wanted" and "taken care of." They were also the least likely to feel "sad," "anxious or worried," "scared or afraid," or "guilty" about sex.[18]

SNAPSHOT 3
Married people reap financial rewards.

- A 2002 study of over 12,000 adults age 51 and older found that individuals in life-long marriages accumulate greater wealth than do unmarried people, who experience a 63 percent reduction in total wealth relative to the married. Separated people experience the greatest reduction in wealth (77 percent), followed by the never married (75 percent), divorced (73 percent), cohabiting (58 percent) and widowed (45 percent).[19]

- A 2002 study found that married men earn about 22 percent more than do men who have never cohabited and never married. The longer men are married, the more their wages increase. Wages rise 6 percent during the first year of marriage, 16 percent by the fifth year, and 24 percent by the tenth year.[20]

- A 2000 study found that both men with shotgun weddings and married men without a premarital conception earn significantly more (15-16 percent) than do never-married men. Because shotgun weddings are likely to be random, this suggests that selection—the possibility that men with higher earning potential are more likely to marry—has little impact on the marriage premium. According to the authors of the study, about 90 percent of the marriage premium remains after controlling for selection.[21]

- Harvard sociologist Elizabeth Gorman determined in 1999 that married men earn more than single men by about 15 percent. Married men also establish higher income goals to support their wives and families. "Married men are more likely to quit with a new job in hand, less likely to quit without having found a new job, and less likely to be terminated involuntarily," found Gorman.[22]

Once married, men earn more, work more, and achieve more. . . . They are more likely to participate in organized, formal relationships governed by clear standards of performance and membership (e.g., church).

—Dr. Steven Nock
Marriage in Men's Lives

Snapshot 4
Women are safer in marriage.

- In a 2002 study, cohabiting couples reported rates of physical aggression in their relationships that were three times higher than those reported by married couples.[23]

- In a 2000 Department of Justice report, married and widowed women had the lowest rates of violent abuse by an intimate. Divorced and separated women had the highest rates of violent abuse by their spouse, ex-spouse, or boyfriend, followed by never-married women.[24]

- Violent abuse rates by a spouse or boyfriend were four times higher among never-married women than were those for married women. Among divorced and separated women, the rate of violent abuse by a spouse, ex-spouse or boyfriend was 12 times greater than that of married women.[25]

- According to the U.S. Department of Justice, nearly half of all family violence is committed by boyfriends, girlfriends, or ex-spouses; only 25 percent is attributed to spouses.[26]

- Married and widowed people are the least likely to be victims of violent crime. Never-married people are the most likely to be a violent crime victim, followed by the divorced and separated.[27]

When you marry, the public commitment you make changes the way you think about yourself and your beloved; it changes the way you act and think about the future; and it changes how other people and other institutions treat you as well.

—Linda Waite and Maggie Gallagher
The Case for Marriage: Why Married People Are Happier, Healthier, and Better Off Financially

WHAT THE POLLS SAY ABOUT MARRIAGE

SNAPSHOT 1
Americans highly value successful marriages.

- In 2000, 81 percent of adults surveyed said that having a good marriage is absolutely necessary for them to consider their life a success.

Question: "How important is having a good marriage for you to consider your life a success?"*

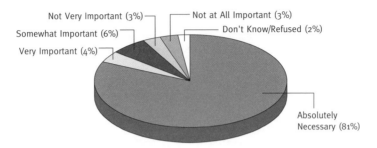

Not Very Important (3%) — Not at All Important (3%)

Somewhat Important (6%) — Don't Know/Refused (2%)

Very Important (4%)

Absolutely Necessary (81%)

Source: Money and the American Family Survey [28]
See endnote for full question.

- For the past twenty-five years, an overwhelming majority of high school seniors have consistently said that having a good marriage and family life is very important to them.

Question: "How important is it to you to have a good marriage and family life?"

Percent Who Said Marriage and Family Life Is Quite or Extremely Important

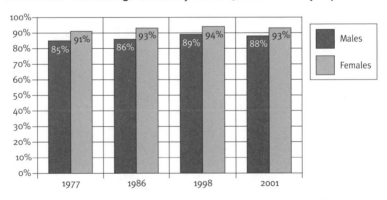

Source: Monitoring the Future Study [29]

SNAPSHOT 2
Americans think that the institution of marriage has been weakened, and they support efforts to strengthen it.

- According to a 1999 poll, a majority believe that the institution of marriage is growing weaker.

Question: "Regarding commitment to marriage, please tell me whether you think that in the past 10 years we have gotten stronger or weaker as a nation."*

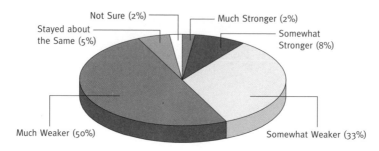

Not Sure (2%)
Stayed about the Same (5%)
Much Stronger (2%)
Somewhat Stronger (8%)
Much Weaker (50%)
Somewhat Weaker (33%)

Source: Shell Poll [30]
See endnote for full question.

- A majority of Americans believe that those who marry today do not take the institution of marriage as seriously as their parents' generation did.

Question: "How seriously do you think most Americans getting married today take the institution of marriage as compared to their parent's generation?"

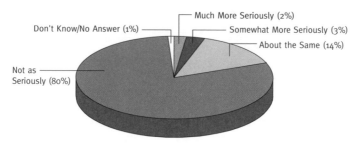

Much More Seriously (2%)
Don't Know/No Answer (1%)
Somewhat More Seriously (3%)
About the Same (14%)
Not as Seriously (80%)

Source: CBS News [31]

- Most young adults strongly support marriage preparation for engaged couples.

Question: "What is your opinion of the importance of individuals or couples consciously preparing for marriage?"

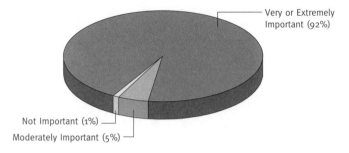

Very or Extremely
Important (92%)

Not Important (1%)
Moderately Important (5%)

Source: Brigham Young University [32]

Snapshot 3

Both nationally and worldwide, people continue to define marriage as a union between one man and one woman.

- A 1999 Wirthlin Worldwide survey conducted for the World Congress of Families II found that 84 percent of people around the world agree that "the definition of marriage is one man and one woman."[33]

- A 2004 Gallup poll showed that a strong majority of adults disapprove of recognizing "gay marriage" in the law.

Question: "Do you think marriages between homosexuals should or should not be recognized by the law as valid, with the same rights as traditional marriages?"

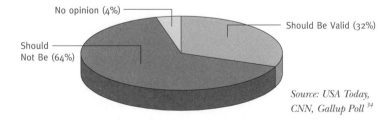

No opinion (4%)

Should Be Valid (32%)

Should
Not Be (64%)

*Source: USA Today,
CNN, Gallup Poll* [34]

- According to a 2004 *CBS News* poll, a majority of Americans oppose homosexual marriage.

Question: "Would you favor or oppose a law allowing homosexuals to marry, giving them the same legal rights as other married couples?"

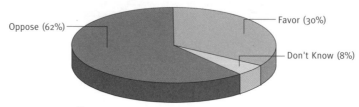

Oppose (62%)

Favor (30%)

Don't Know (8%)

Source: CBS News Poll [35]

CHAPTER 2

The Family

The natural family is the fundamental unit, inscribed in human nature and centered around the voluntary union of a man and a woman in a lifelong covenant of marriage for the purposes of:

- *satisfying the longings of the human heart to give and receive love;*
- *welcoming and ensuring the full physical and emotional development of children;*
- *sharing a home that serves as the center for social, educational, economic, and spiritual life;*
- *building strong bonds among the generations to pass on a way of life that has transcendent meaning; and*
- *extending a hand of compassion to individuals and households whose circumstances fall short of these ideals.*

—World Congress of Families II, Geneva 1999
A Call from the Families of the World

BY THE NUMBERS: THE STATE OF THE FAMILY

SNAPSHOT 1
The majority of households with children under 18 are headed by married couples.

- Among families with children under 18 in 2002, 72 percent were headed by married couples, while 28 percent were headed by single parents.

- The percentage of families with married parents has fallen consistently since 1960, when 91 percent of families with children under 18 were headed by married couples.

Families with Children under 18, by Marital Status, Historical

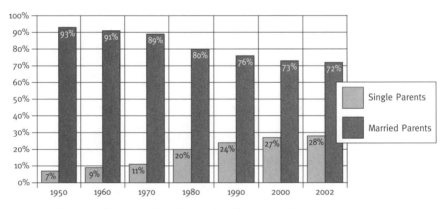

These families may include biological and/or stepfamilies.
Source: U.S. Census Bureau [36]

SNAPSHOT 2
The majority of children live with married parents.

- In 2002, 69 percent of children under age 18 lived with married parents.

Children's Living Arrangements, 2002

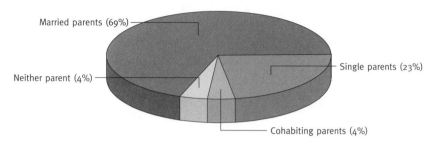

Married parents (69%)

Single parents (23%)

Neither parent (4%)

Cohabiting parents (4%)

Married parents includes biological, adoptive or stepparents.
Source: U.S. Census Bureau [37]

Children's Living Arrangements, 1996

	TOTAL	WHITE NON-HISPANIC	BLACK NON-HISPANIC	OTHER NON-HISPANIC	HISPANIC
Number of Children, Under Age 18	71,494,000	46,657,000	11,033,000	3,377,000	10,428,000
Living with Married Parents	**68.8%**	**77.4%**	**34.8%**	**77.3%**	**63.5%**
• Married Biological or Adoptive Parents	62.4%	70.1%	29.9%	72.7%	58.7%
• Biological/Adoptive Parent Married to Stepparent	6.4%	7.3%	4.9%	4.6%	4.8%
Living with Unmarried Parent(s)	**27.5%**	**20%**	**56.9%**	**19.6%**	**32.0%**
• Single Parent*	22.9%	16%	52.2%	16.2%	24.8%
• Biological Parent(s) Cohabiting	4.6%	4%	4.7%	3.4%	7.2%
Living with No Parents	**3.7%**	**2.5%**	**8.2%**	**3.2%**	**4.3%**

Single parent can be biological parent or stepparent.
Source: U.S. Census Bureau [38]

SNAPSHOT 3

The percentage of children living with married parents dropped dramatically between 1960 and 1995, then leveled off around 1995.

- In 1960, 87.7 percent of children under 18 lived with married parents. By 1995, that percentage had dropped to 68.7 percent.

- The change in living arrangements between 1960 and 1995 was most dramatic for black children. The rate of black children living with married parents in 1995 (33 percent) was half that of 1960 (67 percent).

- Between 1995 and 2002, the percent of black and Hispanic children living with married parents increased, while the percent of white children living with married parents slightly declined.

Percent of Children Under 18 Living with Married Parents, 1960-2002

Year	Percent of Children Living with Married Parents, All Races	Percent of White Children Living with Married Parents	Percent of Black Children Living with Married Parents	Percent of Hispanic Children Living with Married Parents
1960	87.7%	90.9%	67.0%	N/A
1970	85.2%	89.5%	58.5%	77.7%
1975	80.3%	85.4%	49.4%	N/A
1980	76.7%	82.7%	42.2%	75.4%
1985	73.9%	80.0%	39.5%	67.9%
1990	72.5%	79.0%	37.7%	66.8%
1995	68.7%	75.8%	33.1%	62.9%
2000	69.1%	75.3%	37.6%	65.1%
2002	68.7%	74.5%	38.5%	65.1%

Note: Married parents includes stepparents and adoptive parents.
Source: U.S. Census Bureau [39]

SNAPSHOT 4
Married couples are having fewer children today than they were forty years ago.

- Between 1960 and 2002, the birthrate among married women decreased by 45 percent.

Birthrate for Married Women, 1950-2002

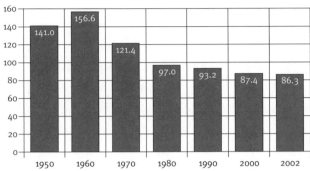

Note: Birthrate is the annual number of births per 1,000 married women age 15-44.
Source: National Center for Health Statistics[40]

- For married parents with children under 18, the average number of children fell from 2.3 in 1960 to 1.9 in 2002, a 17 percent decrease.[41]

- Based on current birth and mortality rates, the total U.S. fertility rate for 2000 was at the replacement level of 2.1 births per woman throughout her lifetime. This was the highest it had been in 30 years.

Total Fertility Rate, 1960-2002

YEAR	TOTAL FERTILITY RATE
1960	3.654
1970	2.480
1980	1.840
1990	2.081
1999	2.075
2000	2.130
2001	2.115
2002	2.013

Note: Total fertility rate is the number of births that a woman would have in her lifetime if, at each year of age, she experienced the birth rate occurring in the specified year.

Source: National Center for Health Statistics[42]

THE BENEFITS OF MARRIED PARENTS

The two-parent family ideal . . . would not only ensure that children had access to the time and money of two adults, it also would provide a system of checks and balances that promote[s] quality parenting. The fact that both adults have a biological connection to the child would increase the likelihood that the parents would identify with the child and be willing to sacrifice for that child, and it would reduce the likelihood that either parent would abuse the child.

—Sara McLanahan and Gary Sandefur
Growing Up with a Single Parent: What Hurts, What Helps

SNAPSHOT 1
Children are safer in homes with married parents.

- Married couples are less likely to abort their children. Approximately 83 percent of abortions are obtained by unmarried women; two-thirds are obtained by never-married women.[43]

- Children living with both parents are far less likely to be physically neglected or abused than are children in single-parent homes. A 1996 study of child abuse found that the rate of neglect of children living with single parents was more than twice that of children living with both parents, and the rate of abuse was 35 percent higher for children in single-parent homes.[44]

SNAPSHOT 2
Children in homes with married parents are healthier and less likely to engage in risky behavior.

- A 1998 study found that girls who lived with their married biological parents in eighth grade were only one-third as likely to have a premarital birth by grade 12 than were girls living in other family structures.[45]

- A 1998 national study on drug abuse found that adolescents age 12-17 who live with their biological parents are the least likely to use illicit drugs. Adolescents who live with their father only or with their father and stepmother are the most likely to use marijuana or other illicit drugs.[46]

- According to a Swedish study of almost a million children, children raised by single parents are more than twice as likely as those raised in two-parent homes to suffer from a serious psychiatric disorder, to commit or attempt suicide or to develop an alcohol addiction. Girls from single-parent homes are three times more likely to become addicted to drugs, and boys are four times more likely.[47]

- Compared to children living in two-parent families, children raised by single parents are more likely to be diagnosed with asthma and Attention Deficit Hyperactivity Disorder (ADHD). They are also more likely to have missed 11 or more days of school during the prior year due to illness or injury. Also, children in single-parent families were twice as likely to have a learning disability, to have two or more visits to the emergency room in the past year and to be unable to obtain proper medical care, according to the 2001 National Health Interview Survey.[48]

SNAPSHOT 3
Children in married-parent households fare better economically.

- Children living with married parents are less likely to live in poverty. In 2001, 8 percent of children in married-couple families were living in poverty, compared to 39 percent of those living with their mother only.[49]

- In 2001, the median income of a married couple with one or more children under 18 was $65,203, compared to $21,997 for a single mother with at least one child under 18.[50]

Snapshot 4

Children living with married parents experience greater educational success.

- A 2003 study of 11 industrialized countries found that children living in single-parent families have lower math and science scores than do children in two-parent families. The correlation between single parenthood and low test scores was strongest among children in the United States and New Zealand.[51]

- A Taiwanese study of over 50,000 families found that children raised in two-parent families are more likely to attend college than are those raised in single-parent families. Children raised by their father only are 57 percent less likely to attend college than are those raised by both parents. Also, two-parent families spend significantly more on their children's education than do single-parent families.[52]

Snapshot 5

Parent-child relationships are better in homes where parents are married.

- Children living with their married biological parents spend more time with their fathers and receive more affection and warmth from them than do those living with a step- or single father or a cohabiting father figure.[53]

- Children living with both biological parents spend more time with their mothers and fathers than do children living with a single parent.[54]

Snapshot 6

Children raised by married parents are less likely to cohabit and more likely to have stable marriages.

- A national study of two generations found that children with continuously married parents are 50 percent less likely to divorce than are children of divorce.[55]

- A fifteen-year national study found that children with married parents are less likely to cohabit or to divorce than are those with divorced parents.[56]

WHAT THE POLLS SAY ABOUT FAMILIES

SNAPSHOT 1
Around the world, a family formed by marriage is seen as the foundation of society.

- In 1999, 78 percent of people surveyed worldwide agreed that "a family created through lawful marriage is the fundamental unit of society."[57]

- In 2000, 92 percent of Americans agreed that "families stand at the center of our society. We can only go forward in this country if families and family values are strengthened."[58]

SNAPSHOT 2
There is strong global and national agreement that it is best for children to be raised by a married mother and father.

- In 1999, 86 percent of people worldwide agreed that "all things being equal, it is better for children to be raised in a household that has a married mother and father."[59]

- Eighty-seven percent of Americans agree that it is best for children to grow up in two-parent homes.

Question: "Please tell me if you agree or disagree with the following statement on family and child rearing: It is generally best for children to grow up in two-parent homes. Agree strongly, agree somewhat, disagree somewhat, disagree strongly?"

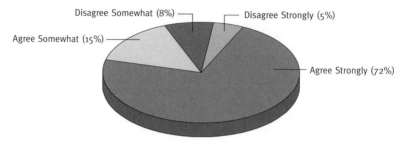

Disagree Somewhat (8%)

Disagree Strongly (5%)

Agree Somewhat (15%)

Agree Strongly (72%)

Source: Public Agenda [60]

- Americans overwhelmingly favor children being raised in a family with a married father and mother, as opposed to a homosexual household.

Question: "As you may know, homosexuals are pressing to adopt children. Which of the following statements best reflects your point of view on this issue?
- **Children are best in mother- and father-based families.**
- **It makes no difference whatsoever whether children are raised by mother and father families or by homosexual families.**
- **Children are best in homosexual families."**

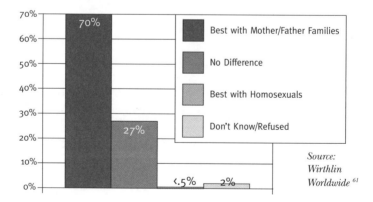

Best with Mother/Father Families

No Difference

Best with Homosexuals

Don't Know/Refused

70%

27%

<.5%   2%

Source: Wirthlin Worldwide [61]

SNAPSHOT 3

Americans believe parents today are doing moderately well at raising their children. They also see value-formation as more challenging than maintaining children's physical well-being.

- In a 2000 poll, nearly half of respondents said parents were doing a fair job of raising children today.

Question: "These days, how good a job are parents doing of raising their children? Overall, would you say they are doing an excellent, good, fair or poor job?"

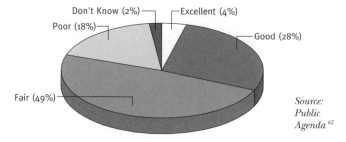

Don't Know (2%) — Excellent (4%)
Poor (18%) —
Good (28%)
Fair (49%) —

Source: Public Agenda [62]

- According to respondents in a 2000 poll, it is more difficult for parents today to raise well-behaved children with good values than it is to provide for children's health and physical well being.

Question: "Which do you think is harder for parents to do these days? To provide for their children's health and physical well being, [or] to raise children who are well behaved and have good values."

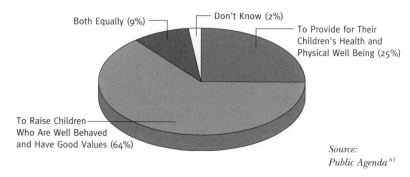

Both Equally (9%) — Don't Know (2%)
To Provide for Their Children's Health and Physical Well Being (25%)
To Raise Children Who Are Well Behaved and Have Good Values (64%)

Source: Public Agenda [63]

SNAPSHOT 4

Most Americans desire to have children and consider raising children a joy.

- In a 2003 survey, 86 percent of adults who do not have children said they want to have children someday.

Question: "Do you want to have children someday, or not?"

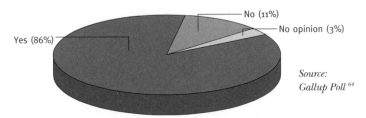

Yes (86%)
No (11%)
No opinion (3%)

Source:
Gallup Poll [64]

- A 1999 poll showed that family and children were most frequently cited as the most fulfilling aspects of life.

  When asked, "What aspect of your life is most fulfilling or satisfying?," 46 percent of respondents said family or children, while eight percent said work and five percent said social life or friends. [65]

- A 2002 poll found that 84 percent of those surveyed believe that watching children grow up is life's greatest joy.

Question: "To what extent do you disagree or agree ... watching children grow up is life's greatest joy?"

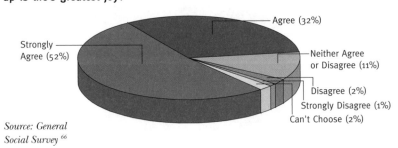

Strongly Agree (52%)
Agree (32%)
Neither Agree or Disagree (11%)
Disagree (2%)
Strongly Disagree (1%)
Can't Choose (2%)

Source: General Social Survey [66]

SNAPSHOT 5

The majority of men highly value marriage and family; similarly, most women consider motherhood an important part of their identity.

- In a 2003 national survey, the majority of men defined success as "being a great father and husband" (87 percent), "having a happy and loving marriage" (85 percent) and "raising happy, successful children" (85 percent).[67]

- In a two-year survey of over 3,300 women, 83 percent said being a mother is a very important part of who they are.[68]

SNAPSHOT 6

The majority of Americans favor expanding tax credits for families with children and think these tax credits will help the economy.

- In a 2003 poll, 86 percent of those surveyed favored expanding tax credits for families.

"Please say whether you favor or oppose the following proposal as part of an economic stimulus bill . . . . Expanding tax credits for families with children."

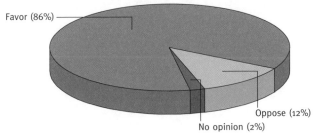

Favor (86%)

Oppose (12%)

No opinion (2%)

Source: Gallup, CNN, USA Today Poll [69]

- A 2003 poll found that 70 percent of Americans believe that expanding tax credits for families with children will help the economy.

"Please say whether you think it will mostly—help the economy, hurt the economy or not make a difference .... Expanding tax credits for families with children."

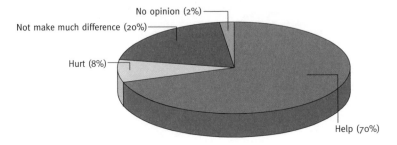

Source: Gallup, CNN, USA Today Poll [70]

CHAPTER 3

Adoption

Here's what I love about adoption: It reveals the good heart of America. . . . Extending the welcome of family to a vulnerable child is a great commitment, but it's an extraordinary act of love. Adoptive families and foster families deserve our nation's thanks, and our nation's recognition.

—President George W. Bush

BY THE NUMBERS: ADOPTION

SNAPSHOT 1
One percent of children in America live with an adoptive mother and father.

Children Living with an Adoptive Mother and Father, 1996

	ADOPTED CHILDREN, ALL RACES	ADOPTED WHITE CHILDREN	ADOPTED BLACK CHILDREN	ADOPTED HISPANIC CHILDREN	ADOPTED AM. INDIAN & ALASKA NATIVE CHILDREN	ADOPTED ASIAN AND PACIFIC ISLANDER CHILDREN
CHILDREN UNDER 18 (71,494,000)	702,000	496,000	45,000	38,000	35,000	88,000
PERCENT OF ALL ADOPTED CHILDREN (702,000)	100%	70.7%	6.4%	5.4%	5.0%	12.5%
PERCENT OF CHILDREN LIVING WITH MARRIED PARENTS, BY RACE (49,186,000)	1.4%	1.2%	1.1%	0.6%	5.8%	4.1%

Source: U.S. Census Bureau [71]

- Among white children living with married parents, the percentage living with adopted parents is 1.2 percent. The proportion is roughly the same (1.1 percent) for black children.

- According to the 2000 Census, 2.5 percent (1.6 million) of children under 18 in the United States are adopted, including those adopted by relatives, non-relatives, and stepparents.[72]

SNAPSHOT 2
Since 1973, a decreasing number of children have been placed for adoption by unmarried women.

- Before 1973, about nine percent of babies born to never-married mothers were placed for adoption, compared to just one percent between 1989 and 1995.

Percent of Out-of-Wedlock Babies Placed for Adoption, 1973-1995

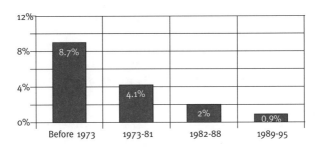

Source: National Center for Health Statistics [73]

- Among white babies born to unwed mothers, the adoption rate has declined even more dramatically: before 1973, nearly 20 percent were placed for adoption, while only 1.7 percent were placed between 1989 and 1995.

Percent of White Out-of-Wedlock Babies Placed for Adoption, 1973-1995

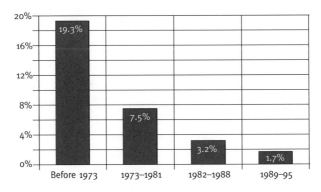

Source: National Center for Health Statistics [74]

SNAPSHOT 3

In the 1990s, the number of infant, foster care and international adoptions increased.

- In 1996, there were 23,537 domestic infant adoptions. In 2000, according the Census Bureau, there were 41,795 adopted children under age one.[75]

- In 2002, 51,000 children were adopted from the public foster care system, compared to 37,000 in 1998.[76]

- In 2001, the State Department issued 20,099 visas to foreign-born children entering the United States, compared to 16,363 in 1998.[77]

SNAPSHOT 4

One out of four married women has considered adoption.

- In 1995, nearly 10 million of the 37.4 million ever-married women age 18-44 had considered adoption.

- About two percent of those who have ever considered adoption are currently taking steps toward adopting.

Ever-Married Women* Who Have Considered Adoption, 1995

Married* Women...	Number	Percent of Women Ever Considering Adoption
...Who Have Ever Considered Adoption	9,893,000	100%
...Seeking, Planning or Would Consider Adoption in Future	5,623,000	56.8%
...Who Would Still Consider, Not Currently Seeking or Planning	5,151,000	52.1%
...Currently Seeking or Planning, Have Not Taken Steps	240,000	2.4%
...Currently Seeking or Planning, Have Taken Steps	232,000	2.3%

*"Ever-married women" means women who are currently or were previously married.
Source: National Center for Health Statistics [78]

SNAPSHOT 5

Although most women seek to adopt an infant, more than one-third of adoption-seeking women are willing to adopt a child age 13 or older.

- In 1995, 37 percent of women seeking to adopt said they would accept a child age 13 or older, while 56.4 percent said they would be willing to adopt a child between age six and 12.

Percent of Women Seeking to Adopt Who Would Accept a Child ...

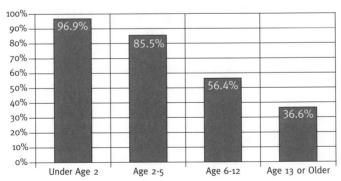

Source: National Center for Health Statistics [79]

THE BENEFITS OF ADOPTION

SNAPSHOT 1
Adoption benefits children.

- A 1998 study of twins separated in childhood (one raised by biological parents and the other by adoptive parents) found that adopted adults experienced a higher socioeconomic environment in childhood, attained higher levels of education and were less likely to drink excessively, compared to those raised in biological families. Adopted adults did have higher incidences of anxiety and social isolation, but according to the study, "their functioning was well within normal limits."[80]

- Among illegitimately born children, those raised in adoptive families scored higher on reading and math tests at age 7 and general ability tests at age 11 than did those not placed for adoption. Also, adopted children had lower rates of learning disabilities and attained higher levels of education by age 33. Compared to birth parents and parents in the general population, adoptive parents showed the most interest in their child's education, which, according to the researchers, was one of the strongest predictors of children's academic achievement.[81]

- According to a Census Bureau report, adopted children are more likely to have better educated parents than are biological children or stepchildren. In 2000, one-third of adoptive parents had a bachelor's, graduate or professional degree, compared to 26 percent of biological parents and 16 percent of step parents.[82]

- The rate of school failure, suspension or expulsion for adopted adolescents is similar to that of children living with both biological parents and is much lower than that of children living with their unmarried mothers or grandparents. Compared to children living with single mothers, adopted children are half as likely to repeat a grade and one-third as likely to be suspended or expelled.[83]

- The largest adoption study to date found that adopted adolescents' self-esteem is as high or higher than their peers'. When compared to a national sample, a greater percentage of adopted children reported little or no anxiety and a positive outlook on the future.[84]

- Adopted children have better health than that of children living either with unmarried mothers or with their grandparents and have access to medical care similar to that of children living with their biological parents.[85]

SNAPSHOT 2
Adoption benefits unwed mothers.

- A 1988 study found that unwed adolescent mothers who place their babies for adoption are less likely than are those who keep their babies to have another out-of-wedlock pregnancy.[86]

- An unwed mother who chooses adoption is more likely to be employed at six and 12 months after giving birth and to earn a higher household income.[87]

- A 1997 study evaluating young women four years after giving birth as unwed teenagers found that mothers who placed their children for adoption were more likely to complete high school, to attend college, to be employed and to get married. They were less likely to be on welfare or to be cohabiting.[88]

- Unwed teenage mothers who place their children for adoption express greater overall satisfaction with their lives, including work, finances and relationships. They are more likely to be optimistic about the future and less likely to suffer from depression.[89]

SNAPSHOT 3
Adoption benefits adoptive parents.

- A study of families who adopted infants between 1974 and 1980 found that divorce and separation were much less common among the parents of adopted adolescents (11 percent) than among non-adoptive parents (28 percent).[90]

- Adoptive and biological parents hold similar respect for marriage and place the same importance on having a mother at home with children under age five, according to a 1998 study.[91]

- A 2004 study found that, compared to parents who recently gave birth, adoptive parents who recently adopted reported higher life satisfaction, fewer spousal disagreements, less depression, higher satisfaction with family life and greater family cohesion.[92]

- In a 1998 study comparing biological and adoptive parents, both groups of parents gave frequent positive affirmation to their children, invested similar amounts of time in their children's lives and attached the same importance to encouraging good behaviors in their children.[93]

- Adoptive parents report levels of self-esteem and general well being just as favorable as those of biological parents, with no greater incidence of depression.[94]

WHAT THE POLLS SAY ABOUT ADOPTION

SNAPSHOT 1
Americans view adoption favorably.

- In a 2000 survey, nearly four out five Americans said they would consider adopting a child.

Question: "Would you consider adopting a child?"

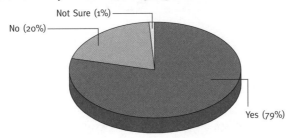

Source: Time, CNN [95]

- A 2002 survey found that nearly two-thirds (63 percent) of Americans have a very favorable opinion about adoption, 31 percent have a somewhat favorable opinion and only 5 percent have an unfavorable opinion.[96]

SNAPSHOT 2
A majority of Americans think adoptive parents will love their adopted children as much as their biological children.

- In a 2002 survey, 75 percent of respondents said it is very likely that adoptive parents will love their adoptive children as much as their biological children.

Question: "How likely is it that parents who adopt children will love them as much as they would have loved children they gave birth to?"

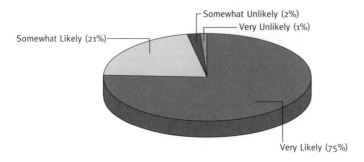

Source: Harris Interactive [97]

- A 2002 survey found that 86 percent of Americans believe that adoptive parents experience the same amount or more satisfaction from raising an adopted child as they do from raising a biological child.

Question: "Do you think parents get the same amount of satisfaction out of raising an adopted child as raising a child born to them, more satisfaction, or less satisfaction?"

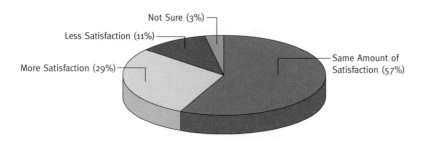

Source: Harris Interactive [98]

SNAPSHOT 3
Americans support public policies that promote adoption.

- Sixty-three percent of adults surveyed in 2000 approved of increasing tax incentives for adoptions.

Question: "Please tell me if you approve or disapprove of increasing tax incentives for adoptions."

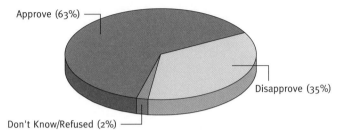

Approve (63%)

Disapprove (35%)

Don't Know/Refused (2%)

Source: Wirthlin Worldwide [99]

- In 1997, 67 percent said they support pro-adoption policies for pregnant teens on welfare.

Question: "Should pregnant teenagers who receive welfare be encouraged to put their babies up for adoption? Do you strongly support, somewhat support, somewhat oppose or strongly oppose it?"

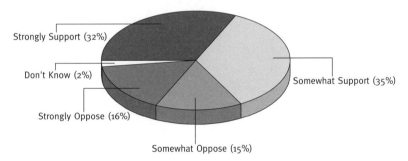

Strongly Support (32%)

Don't Know (2%)

Strongly Oppose (16%)

Somewhat Oppose (15%)

Somewhat Support (35%)

Source: Princeton Survey Research [100]
*See endnotes for full question.

CHAPTER 4

The Care of Children

There is an emptiness in the soul of woman under ecstatic capitalism. The office, with its ephemeral projects, water-cooler intimacies, and disposable employees, cannot satisfy the hunger for enduring connections, for the happiness that comes from the passionate love stirred by an utterly dependent being, for knowing and being known in ways only possible in the private space of family life.

—Kay Hymowitz
"Fear and Loathing at the
Day Care Center"
City Journal, Summer 2001

BY THE NUMBERS: CHILD CARE

SNAPSHOT 1
Over half of all mothers with young children either do not work outside the home or are employed part time.

- In 2001, a majority of women with children under age six were employed part time or not at all; 42 percent were employed full time.

Employment Status of Mothers of Children under Age Six*, 2001

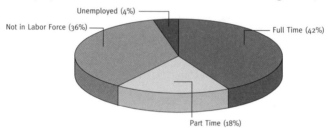

Unemployed (4%)

Not in Labor Force (36%)

Full Time (42%)

Part Time (18%)

*Total number of women with children under age six is 15,986,000. Part time means working less than 35 hours a week at all jobs. Full time means working 35 hours or more a week at all jobs.

Source: Bureau of Labor Statistics [101]

- In 2002, 45 percent of mothers with infants were not in the labor force, 34 percent worked full-time, 16 percent worked part time and 5 percent were unemployed.

Employment Status of Mothers of Infants, 2002

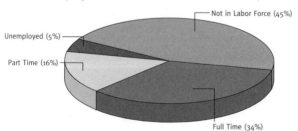

Not in Labor Force (45%)

Unemployed (5%)

Part Time (16%)

Full Time (34%)

*Not in the labor force means not working and not looking for work.
**Unemployed means not working, but looking for work.
Source: U.S. Census Bureau [102]

SNAPSHOT 2
Since 1998, more mothers of infants have chosen not to work.

- After years of increasing participation in the labor force, the rate of working mothers of infants declined from 59 percent in 1998 to 55 percent in 2002.

Labor Force Participation of Mothers of Children 12 Months and Younger, 1978-2002

Year	NUMBER OF WOMEN AGE 15-44 WITH CHILDREN UNDER 12 MONTHS	PERCENT IN THE LABOR FORCE
1978*	3,168,000	35%
1980*	3,247,000	38%
1984*	3,311,000	47%
1988*	3,667,000	51%
1990*	3,913,000	53%
1994	3,890,000	53%
1998	3,671,000	59%
2000	3,934,000	55%
2002	3,766,000	55%

*Women 18 to 44 years old; statistics for other years based on women 15 to 44 years old.
Source: U.S. Census Bureau [103]

SNAPSHOT 3
Only half of children under age 5 have an employed mother.

- Of those children under age 5 with an employed mother, one-third have a mother who works part time.

- Among children under age 5 with an unemployed mother, 86 percent have mothers who are not looking for work and are not in school.

Employment Status of Mothers with Children under Age 5, 1997

Total Number of Children Under Age 5*	Children with an Employed Mother	Children with an Unemployed Mother
19,195,000 100%	10,116,000 53%	9,079,000 47%

Includes only children living with their single or married mother. Children living with father only are excluded from this number.

Source: U.S. Census Bureau [104]

- The number of children under age 15 with a stay-at-home mother and an employed father increased from 9.3 million in 1994 to 11 million in 2002—an 18 percent increase.[105]

SNAPSHOT 4

Fifty percent of children under age 5 with an employed mother are cared for by their parents, grandparents or other relatives.

- Only one-fifth of children under age 5 with employed mothers are placed in a day care facility or preschool.

Primary Child Care Arrangements for Children under Age Five, 1999

Total Number of Children Under Age 5 with an Employed Mother	Children Cared for by Father or by Mother at work	Children Cared for by Grandparent or Relative	Children Cared for by Family Friend or Neighbor	Children in Day Care Facility or Preschool	Children in Other Arrangements
10,587,000	21.5%	28.8%	20.3%	22.1%	7.3%

Source: U.S. Census Bureau [106]

SNAPSHOT 5

Employed mothers consistently choose care by relatives or family friends over day care centers.

Primary Child Care Arrangements for Children under Age Five, 1977-1999

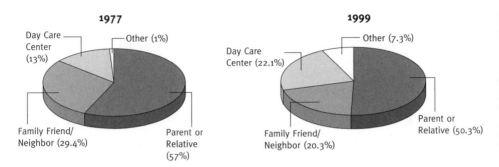

1977

Day Care Center (13%)
Other (1%)
Family Friend/ Neighbor (29.4%)
Parent or Relative (57%)

1999

Day Care Center (22.1%)
Other (7.3%)
Family Friend/ Neighbor (20.3%)
Parent or Relative (50.3%)

Year	Number of Children Under Age Five in Child Care	Percent Cared for by Father at Home or by Mother at Work*	Percent Cared for by Grandparent or Other Relative	Percent Cared for by Family Friend or Neighbor	Percent Placed in Day Care Center or Pre-School	Other
1977	4,370,000	25.8%	30.9%	29.4%	13.0%	1.0%
1985	8,168,000	23.8%	24.1%	28.2%	23.1%	0.8%
1988	9,483,000	22.7%	21.1%	28.9%	25.8%	1.4%
1990	9,629,000	22.9%	23.1%	25.1%	27.5%	1.2%
1991	9,854,000	28.7%	23.5%	23.3%	23.0%	1.6%
1993	9,937,000	22.1%	25.3%	21.6%	30.1%	1.1%
1994	10,288,000	24.0%	25.3%	20.5%	29.4%	1.1%
1995	10,047,000	22.0%	21.4%	28.4%	25.1%	2.9%
1997	10,116,000	22.3%	25.8%	22.1%	21.7%	8.1%
1999	10,587,000	21.5%	28.8%	20.3%	22.1%	7.3%

*Mother cares for child while working for pay at home or away from home.

Source: U.S. Census Bureau [107]

THE EFFECTS OF DAY CARE ON CHILDREN

SNAPSHOT 1
Early and extensive day care affects children's behavior negatively.

- A 2003 national study which followed children from birth through the first four-and-a-half years of life found that the more time children spent in day care, the more likely they were to be assertive, aggressive and disobedient at age four-and-a-half and in kindergarten. The link between large amounts of time in day care and increased aggression and disobedience persists, even after taking into account maternal sensitivity and family background as well as the quality, type, and instability of child care.[108]

- A 10-year study released in 2001 found that children age four-and-a-half who experienced an average of more than 30 hours per week in day care exhibited more behavior problems than did those who spent under 10 hours per week in day care, even after making adjustments for the quality of the care.[109]

- Child-care expert Dr. Jay Belsky found that children who experience "early and extensive non-maternal care" during their first year of life are less likely to develop secure infant-parent bonding than are infants who experience extensive maternal care. These children are also at risk for showing elevated levels of aggression and noncompliance between ages three and eight.[110]

SNAPSHOT 2
Extensive day care negatively affects children's social adjustment and cognitive development.

- A 1999 study found poor cognitive development and academic achievement in children whose mothers worked outside the home during their first three years. Working more hours was associated with lower academic achievement scores before age seven and lower cognitive development scores before age nine.[111]

- A 1998 study of five year-olds' behavior during play time found that those who experienced little or no day care were more likely to be polite, smile and to offer to help the other child, compared to those who spent more time in daycare. According to the author, "the most prosocial children were those who had never attended daycare."[112]

- A 2002 NICHD study found that when mothers were employed by the time their children were nine months old, children scored lower on cognitive development tests at age three. Children's cognitive development at this age was impacted more negatively when their mothers worked 30 hours or more a week.[113]

SNAPSHOT 3
Mother-child interaction is less positive for children who have spent considerable time in day care.

- A 1999 National Institute of Child Health and Human Development (NICHD) study found that increased weekly hours of day care were a predictor for less maternal sensitivity and less positive mother-child interaction. Researchers studying children from six months to three years found that children who spent more than 10 hours a week in day care interacted less positively with their mothers than did those who spent fewer hours in day care. For children in day care centers more than 10 hours per week, the fewer hours spent in day care, the more positive their engagement with their mothers.[114]

- A 1997 NICHD study found that children were less securely attached to their mothers when they experienced low maternal sensitivity and more than 10 hours per week in day care. Children became more attached to their mother by spending more time with her.[115]

SNAPSHOT 4:
Children in day care facilities have greater health risks and higher health care costs.

- According to a 1999 *Pediatrics* study, children placed in day care centers were at greater risk of contracting invasive pneumococcal disease, such as pneumonia or meningitis, than those who were cared for at home. Children in day care were nearly twice as likely to have had a recent ear infection and three times as likely to have had a recent course of antibiotics.[116]

- A study of children in 59 day care centers in Toronto, Ontario, found a high prevalence of Streptococcus pneumoniae, one of the most common upper-respiratory pathogens causing ear infections, pharyngitis and pneumonia. Forty-four percent of the 1,322 children studied tested positive for this bacteria, which was found in all except one of the day care centers.[117]

- A 2003 study of 67 children attending full-time day care at one of four centers revealed elevated levels of cortisol, a stress hormone, among one-third of the infants and 71 percent of the toddlers. Researchers found that a majority of the children had decreased cortisol levels on the days they were cared for at home.[118]

- A 1999 study found that three- to five-year-old children in day care are at increased risk of developing upper respiratory infections. Those who started day care at an early age were at increased risk of recurrent ear infections and asthma.[119]

- Children who attend day care centers are two to three times more likely to visit the emergency room and doctor's office and to use prescription drugs than are children cared for by their parents. Additionally, children attending day care centers have higher annual health care expenditures ($985) than do children who are not in day care ($642).[120]

WHAT THE POLLS SAY ABOUT CHILD CARE

SNAPSHOT 1
Americans think parents' care is the best care for young children.

- A 1998 poll found that Americans rate care by a child's mother as the single most desirable form of care for pre-school children.

Question: "On a scale from 1-10, please rate how desirable each of these pre-school child care options is, with 1 being the least desirable and 10 being the most desirable."

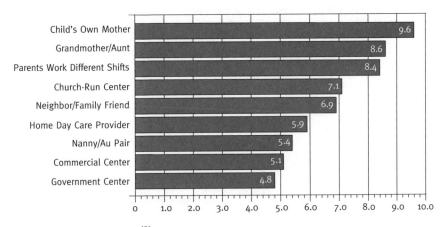

Source: Wirthlin Worldwide [121]

- A 2001 poll found that most Americans do not think it is ideal for both parents to work full time outside the home.

Question: "Which of the following do you see as the ideal situation for a family in today's society:
• one parent stays at home solely to raise children,
• both parents work outside the home: one full time, one part time,
• both parents work: one at home, one outside the home,
• both parents work full time outside the home."

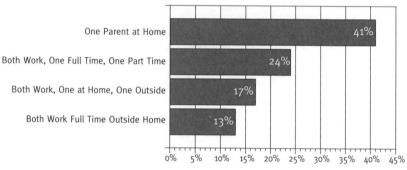

Source: Gallup [122]

• In 2000, 70 percent of parents of children age five and under indicated that having one parent at home is the best care arrangement for the very young.

Question: "Which is the best child care arrangement during a child's earliest years?"

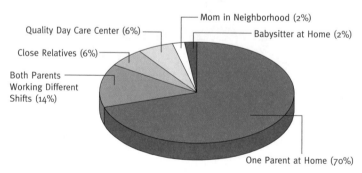

Source: Public Agenda [123]

• In a 2003 poll, 61 percent said children are better off if their mother is home and unemployed, rather than working.

Question: "Do you think children are better off if their mother is home and doesn't hold a job or are the children just as well off if the mother works?"

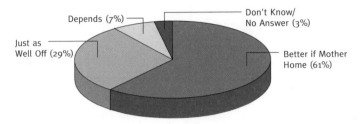

Source: CBS News, New York Times [124]

SNAPSHOT 2

Most Americans do not think day care can adequately substitute for parental care.

- In a 2000 poll, 63 percent of parents with children age five and under did not think that quality day care is an adequate substitute for a stay-at-home parent.

Question: "When children go to a top-notch day care center, the care and attention they get is just as good as what they would get from a stay-at-home parent. Do you agree or disagree?"

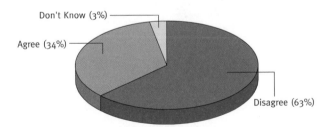

Source: Public Agenda [125]

- In 2000, 71 percent of parents surveyed believed they should rely on day care only if they had no other option.

Question: "Parents should only rely on a day care center when they have no other option."

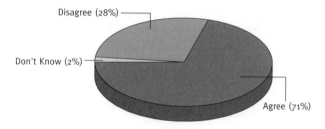

Disagree (28%)

Don't Know (2%)

Agree (71%)

Source: Public Agenda [126]

- According to a 2000 poll, 46 percent of parents surveyed indicated that a day care center was their "least preferred" child care arrangement.

Question: "What is the 'least preferred' arrangement for child care for children under five?"

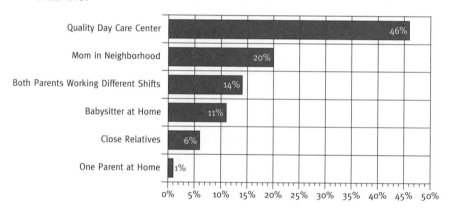

Source: Public Agenda [127]

- Sixty percent of Americans believe that pre-school children are spending too much time in day care programs or with babysitters.

Question: "Concerning placing children in daycare or leaving them with babysitters, has America gone too far or not far enough in this direction?"*

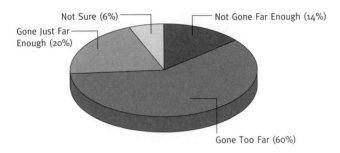

Source: Shell Poll [128]

*See endnote for full question

SNAPSHOT 3
Most mothers of children under 18 prefer their role as a mother to that of a working woman.

- In 1997, a majority of mothers with children under 18 said they find their family relationships more fulfilling to them than their work.

When the Pew Research Center asked mothers with children under 18 about their most important source of personal happiness and fulfillment, 51 percent cited their relationship with their children, 29 percent cited their relationship with their husband or partner, while only one percent cited their job or career.[129]

- Only one-third of mothers with children under 18 said they prefer full-time work to part-time work or none at all.

When mothers of children under 18 were asked in a 1997 poll if, ideally, they would prefer to work full time, part time or not at all, 44 percent said they would prefer to work part time, 30 percent prefer to work full time and 26 percent said they would prefer not to work at all.[130]

SNAPSHOT 4
Americans think that new mothers are pressured to return too quickly to the workforce, and they support tax relief for stay-at-home parents.

- Four out of five parents with children agree that many new mothers are pressured to return to work too quickly.

Question: "Please tell how much you agree or disagree ... These days, too many new moms are under pressure to return to work too quickly after having a child."

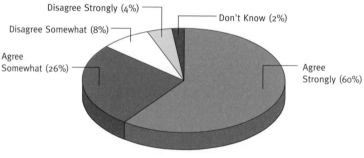

Disagree Strongly (4%)
Don't Know (2%)
Disagree Somewhat (8%)
Agree Somewhat (26%)
Agree Strongly (60%)

Source: Public Agenda [131]

- Most Americans favor offering child care tax credits to families with a stay-at-home parent.

**Question: "Offering child care tax credits to families with a stay-at-home par-
ent—do you favor or oppose that?"**

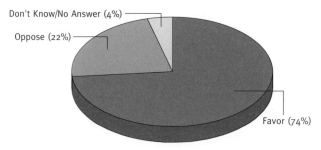

Don't Know/No Answer (4%)

Oppose (22%)

Favor (74%)

Source: CBS News [132]

- In 2000, a majority of parents with children age 5 and under said they support tax breaks for stay-at-home parents.

**Question: "How helpful do you think the following policy proposal would be
as far as improving the care that young children get? .... Giving a much big-
ger tax break to parents who stay home to care for their children".**

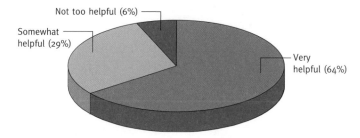

Not too helpful (6%)

Somewhat
helpful (29%)

Very
helpful (64%)

Source: Public Agenda [133]

- According to a 2000 poll, 62 percent of parents with children age 5 and under prefer public policies that make it easier for one parent to stay at home rather than policies for improving the cost and quality of child care.

Question: "Do you think public policies on families and work should focus more on making it easier and more affordable for one parent to stay at home or on improving the cost and quality of child care?"

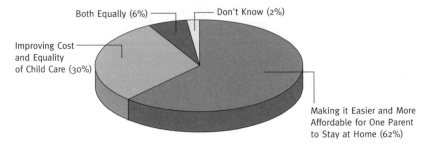

Source: Public Agenda[134]

NOTES

CHAPTER 1 Marriage

1   National Center for Health Statistics, *Monthly Vital Statistics Report,* Vol. 43, No. 12, July 14, 1995, U.S. Census Bureau, *Statistical Abstract of the United States: 2000,* Table 144 and The National Marriage Project, "The State of Our Unions 2003: The Social Health of Marriage in America," June 2003, p. 24, Figure 1.

2   U.S. Census Bureau, "Marital Status of the Population 15 Years Old and Over, by Sex and Race: 1950 to Present," Table MS-1, June 12, 2003. Percent calculations by the author.

3   U.S. Census Bureau, "Estimated Median Age at First Marriage, by Sex: 1890 to the Present," Table MS-2, June 12, 2003.

4   Rose M. Kreider and Tavia Simmons, "Marital Status: 2000," *Census 2000 Brief,* U.S. Census Bureau, October 2003, Table 4.

5   Ibid.

6   Jason Fields, *America's Families and Living Arrangements 2000,* Current Population Reports, P20-537, U.S. Census Bureau, June 2001, Table 5. Percent calculations by the author. Jason Fields, "Children's Living Arrangements and Characteristics: March 2002," *Current Population Reports,* U.S. Census Bureau, June 2003, Detailed Table A1.

7   Steven Stack and Ross Eshleman, "Marital Status and Happiness: A 17-Nation Study," *Journal of Marriage and the Family* 60 (May 1998): 527-536.

8   Nadine F. Marks and James David Lambert, "Marital Status Continuity and Change Among Young and Midlife Adults," *Journal of Family Issues* 19 (November 1998): 652-686.

9   John Cairney and Michael Boyle, et al., "Stress, Social Support and Depression in Single and Married Mothers," *Social Psychiatry and Psychiatric Epidemiology* 38 (August 2003): 442-449.

10 Robin W. Simon, "Revisiting the Relationships Among Gender, Marital Status and Mental Health," *American Journal of Sociology* 107 (January 2002): 1065-1096.

11 Kathleen A. Lamb, et al., "Union Formation and Depression: Selection and Relationship Effects," *Journal of Marriage and Family* 65 (November 2003): 953-962.

12 Robin W. Simon and Kristen Marcussen, "Marital Transitions, Marital Beliefs, and Mental Health," *Journal of Health and Social Behavior* 40 (1999): 111-125.

13 Amy Mehraban Pienta, "Health Consequences of Marriage for the Retirement Years," *Journal of Family Issues* 21 (July 2000): 559-586.

14 Barbara Steinberg Schone and Robin M. Weinick, "Health-Related Behaviors and the Benefits of Marriage for Elderly Persons," *The Gerontologist* 38 (October 1998): 618-627.

15   Augustine J. Kposowa, "Marital Status and Suicide in the National Longitudinal Mortality Study," *Journal of Epidemiology and Community Health* 54 (April 2000): 254-261.

16   Ping Qin, et al., "Suicide Risk in Relation to Socioeconomic, Demographic, Psychiatric and Familial Factors: A National Register-Based Study of All Suicides in Denmark, 1981-1997," *The American Journal of Psychiatry* 160 (April 2003): 765-772.

17   Edward O. Laumann, et al., *The Social Organization of Sexuality: Sexual Practices in the United States* (Chicago: University of Chicago Press, 1994), p. 364.

18   Ibid., p. 368.

19   Janet Wilmoth and Gregor Koso, "Does Marital History Matter? Marital Status and Wealth Outcomes Among Preretirement Adults," *Journal of Marriage and Family* 64 (February 2002): 254-268.

20   Leslie S. Stratton, "Examining the Wage Differential for Married and Cohabiting Men," *Economic Inquiry* 40 (April 2002): 199-212.

21   Donna K. Ginther and Madeline Zavodny, "Is the Male Marriage Premium Due to Selection? The Effect of Shotgun Weddings on the Return to Marriage," *Journal of Population Economics* 14 (2001): 313-328.

22   Elizabeth Gorman, "Bringing Home the Bacon: Marital Allocation of Income-Earning Responsibility, Job-Shifts and Men's Wages," *Journal of Marriage and the Family* 61 (February 1999): 110-122.

23   Sonia Miner Salari and Bret M. Baldwin, "Verbal, Physical, and Injurious Aggression Among Intimate Couples Over Time," *Journal of Family Issues* 23 (May 2002): 523-550.

24   Bureau of Justice Statistics, *Intimate Partner Violence*, National Crime Victimization Survey, U.S. Department of Justice, May 2000, pp. 4-5, 11.

25   Ibid.

26   Bureau of Justice Statistics, *Highlights from 20 Years of Surveying Crime Victims: The National Crime Victimization Survey, 1973-92*, U.S. Department of Justice, September 1993, p. 25.

27   Bureau of Justice Statistics, *Criminal Victimization 1999: Changes 1998-1999 with Trends 1993-99*, National Crime Victimization Survey, U.S. Department of Justice, August 2000, p. 7.

28   Full question reads: "(Please tell me, for you personally, if each of the following is absolutely necessary or not for you to consider your life a success? (If not, ask) How important is it to you for your life to be a success: very important, somewhat important, not very, or not at all important.) ... Having a good marriage." Research, Strategy, Management & Belden Russonello & Stewart for American Association of Retired Persons, January 23 – February 21, 2000.

29   University of Michigan Institute for Social Research, *ISR Update*, Vol. 2, No. 1, Fall 2002.

30   Full question reads: "(I'm going to read you a list of values that some people may feel are important. For each one, please tell me whether you think that in the past ten years we have gotten much stronger as a nation, somewhat stronger as a nation, somewhat weaker as a nation, or much weaker as a nation in terms of this value.)" Peter D. Hart Research Associates for Shell Oil Company, March 16-20, 1999.

31 CBS News Poll, February 10-12, 2001.

32 2001 Survey of 964 college-age young adults at four universities, as cited in S. F. Duncan and M. M. Wood, "Reaching At-risk Audiences with Marriage Preparation Programs," presented at the Annual Meeting of the National Council on Family Relations, Rochester, New York, November 6-11, 2001.

33 Wirthlin Worldwide for The Howard Center and Brigham Young University, World Congress of Families II, November 1999.

34 USA Today, CNN, Gallup Poll, February 2004.

35 CBS News Poll, February 24-27, 2004.

CHAPTER 2 The Family

36 U.S. Bureau of the Census, "Families by Presence of Own Children Under 18: 1950 to Present," Table FM-1, June 12, 2003. Percent calculations by the author.

37 Jason Fields, *Children's Living Arrangements and Characteristics: March 2002*, Current Population Reports P20-547, June 2003, U.S. Census Bureau, Table 1.

38 Jason Fields, *Living Arrangements of Children 1996*, Current Population Reports, P70-74, U.S. Census Bureau, April 2001, Internet Table 1. Percent calculations by the author.

39 U.S. Census Bureau, "Living Arrangements of Children Under 18 Years Old: 1960 to Present," Table CH-1; "Living Arrangements of White Children Under 18 Years Old: 1960 to Present," Table CH-2; "Living Arrangements of Black Children Under 18 Years Old: 1960 to Present," Table CH-3; and "Living Arrangements of Hispanic Children Under 18 Years Old: 1970 to Present," Table CH-4," June 12, 2003, Available at *www.census.gov/population/socdemo/hh-fam.html*; U.S. Census Bureau, "Living Arrangements of Children Under 18 Years and Marital Status of Parents, by Age, Gender Race and Hispanic Origin of the Child for All Children: March 2002," Table C3. Percent calculations by author.

40 Joyce A Martin, et al., *Births: Final Data for 2002*, National Vital Statistics Reports 52, December 17, 2003, Table D, and U.S. Department of Health and Human Services, *Report to Congress on Out-of-Wedlock Childbearing*, September 1995, Table III-7.

41 U.S. Census Bureau, "Average Number of Own Children Under 18 Per Family, by Type of Family: 1955 to Present," Table FM-3, June 12, 2003, Available at *www.census.gov/population/socdemo/hh-fam/tabFM-3.pdf*.

42 National Center for Health Statistics, *Vital Statistics of the United States 1990*, Vol. I – Natality, Hyattsville, Maryland, 1994, Table 1-9, *Statistical Abstract of the United States: 2003*, Table 88 and Joyce A. Martin, et al., *Births: Final Data for 2002*, Table 4.

43 The Alan Guttmacher Institute, "Induced Abortion," *Facts in Brief*, 2003 and Kaiser Family Foundation, *Fact Sheet: Abortion in the U.S.*, January 2003.

44 Andrea J. Sedlak and Diane D. Broadhurst, *The Third National Incidence Study of Child Abuse and Neglect*, U.S. Department of Health and Human Services, 1996, pp. xviii, 5-19.

45 Kristin A. Moore, et al., "Nonmarital School-Age Motherhood: Family, Individual, and School Characteristics," *Journal of Adolescent Research* 13 (October 1998): 433-457.

46   John P. Hoffmann and Robert A. Johnson, "A National Portrait of Family Structure and Adolescent Drug Use," *Journal of Marriage and the Family* 60 (August 1998): 633-645.

47   Gunilla Ringback Weitoft, et al., "Mortality, Severe Morbidity and Injury in Children Living with Single Parents in Sweden: A Population-based Study," *The Lancet* 361 (January 25, 2003): 289-295.

48   Barbara Bloom, et al., *Summary Health Statistics for U.S. Children: National Health Interview Survey, 2001*, National Center for Health Statistics, Vital and Health Statistics, Series 10, No. 216, 2003.

49   Federal Interagency Forum on Child and Family Statistics, *America's Children: Key Indicators of Well-Being 2003*, Washington, D.C., p. 16.

50   U.S. Census Bureau, "Historical Income Tables – Families," Table F-10, September 30, 2002, Available at *www.census.gov/hhes/income/histinc/f10.html.*

51   Suet-Ling Pong, et al., "Family Policies and Children's School Achievement in Single-Versus Two-Parent Families," *Journal of Marriage and Family* 65 (August 2003): 681-699.

52   Wen-Jui Han, et al., "The Importance of Family Structure and Family Income on Family's Educational Expenditure and Children's College Attendance: Empirical Evidence from Taiwan," *Journal of Family Issues* 24 (September 2003): 753-786.

53   Sandra L. Hofferth and Kermyt G. Anderson, "Are All Dads Equal? Biology Versus Marriage as a Basis for Paternal Investment," *Journal of Marriage and Family* 65 (February 2003): 213-232.

54   Sara McLanahan and Gary Sandefur, *Growing Up with a Single Parent: What Hurts, What Helps* (Cambridge: Harvard University Press, 1994), pp. 95-101.

55   Paul R. Amato and Danelle D. DeBoer, "The Transmission of Marital Instability Across Generations: Relationship Skills or Commitment to Marriage?" *Journal of Marriage and Family* 63 (November 2001): 1038-1051.

56   Paul R. Amato and Alan Booth, *A Generation at Risk: Growing Up in an Era of Family Upheaval* (Massachusetts: Harvard University Press, 1997), pp. 111-115.

57   Wirthlin Worldwide for The Howard Center and Brigham Young University, World Congress of Families II, November, 1999.

58   *The Wirthlin Report: Current Trends in Public Opinion from Wirthlin Worldwide*, August 2000.

59   Wirthlin Worldwide for The Howard Center and Brigham Young University, World Congress of Families II, November, 1999.

60   Public Agenda, "Necessary Compromises," June 1-15, 2000.

61   Wirthlin Worldwide for Family Research Council, July 23-26, 1999.

62   Public Agenda, "Necessary Compromises."

63   Ibid.

64   Gallup Poll, July 18 – July 20, 2003.

65   *New York Times* Poll, July 17-19, 1999.

66   General Social Survey, February 6 – June 26, 2002.

67   ManScan survey of 1,300 men, April 2003, conducted for *Men's Health Magazine.*

68   The Center for the Advancement of Women, "Progress and Perils: New Agenda for Women," June 2003.

69   Gallup Organization for CNN and *USA Today,* January 3-5, 2003.

70   Ibid.

CHAPTER 3 Adoption

71   Jason Fields, *Living Arrangements of Children 1996,* Table 2. Percent calculations by the author.

72   Rose M. Kreider, "Adopted Children and Stepchildren: 2000," *Census 2000 Special Reports,* U.S. Census Bureau, August 2003, Table 3.

73   Anjani Chandra, et al., *Adoption, Adoption Seeking, and Relinquishment for Adoption in the United States,* Advance Data No. 306, National Center for Health Statistics, May 11, 1999, p. 9.

74   Ibid.

75   Paul J. Placek, "National Adoption Data," in Connaught Marshner, ed. *Adoption Factbook III,* National Council for Adoption, 1999, p. 41 and Rose M. Kreider, "Adopted Children and Stepchildren: 2000," Table 3.

76   National Adoption and Foster Care Statistics, "Trends in Foster Care and Adoption," Available at *www.acf.hhs.gov/programs/cb/dis/afcars/publications/afcars.htm.*

77   U.S. State Department, "Immigrant Visas Issued to Orphans Coming to the U.S.," Available at *www.travel.state.gov/orphan_numbers.html.*

78   Anjani Chandra, et al., *Adoption, Adoption Seeking, and Relinquishment for Adoption in the United States,* Figure 3.

79   Ibid, Table 4.

80   Michael A. Smyer and Margaret Gatz, et al., "Childhood Adoption: Long-Term Effects in Adulthood," *Psychiatry* (Fall 1998): 191-205.

81   Barbara Maughan, et al., "School Achievement and Adult Qualifications Among Adoptees: A Longitudinal Study," *Journal of Child Psychology and Psychiatry* 39 (1998): 669-685.

82   Rose M. Kreider, "Adopted Children and Stepchildren: 2000," Table 7.

83   Dr. Nicholas Zill, "Adopted Children in the United States: A Profile Based on a National Survey of Child Health," Testimony before the Subcommittee on Human Resources of the Committee on Ways and Means, House of Representatives, Washington, D.C., May 10, 1995.

84   Peter L. Benson, et al., "Growing Up Adopted: A Portrait of Adolescents and Their Families," Search Institute, Minneapolis, June 1994, p. 67.

85   Dr. Nicholas Zill, "Adopted Children in the United States."

86 Steven D. McLaughlin, et al., "Do Adolescents Who Relinquish Their Children Fare Better or Worse Than Those Who Raise Them?" *Family Planning Perspectives* 20 (January-February 1988): 25-32.

87 Ibid., p. 25.

88 Pearila Brickner Namerow, et al., "The Consequences of Placing versus Parenting Among Unmarried Women," *Marriage and Family Review* 25 (1997): 175-197.

89 Ibid.

90 Peter L. Benson, et al., "Growing Up Adopted," p. 45.

91 L. DiAnne Borders, et al., "Are Adopted Children and Their Parents at Greater Risk for Negative Outcomes?" *Family Relations* 47 (1998): 237-241.

92 Rosario Ceballo, et al., "Gaining a Child: Comparing the Experiences of Biological Parents, Adoptive Parents, and Stepparents," *Family Relations* 53 (January 2004): 38-48.

93 L. DiAnne Borders, et al., "Are Adopted Children and Their Parents at Greater Risk for Negative Outcomes?"

94 Ibid.

95 Yankelovich Partners, Inc., for Time, CNN, August 9-10, 2000.

96 Harris Interactive for the Dave Thomas Foundation for Adoption as cited in "National Adoption Attitudes Survey," Dave Thomas Foundation for Adoption, June 2002.

97 Ibid.

98 Ibid.

99 Wirthlin Worldwide for the Alliance for Marriage, July 7-10, 2000.

100 Full question reads: "The same proposal (a plan to encourage welfare recipients to consider putting their children up for adoption) suggests that pregnant teenagers who aren't able to provide for their babies be encouraged to put their babies up for adoption. How do you feel about such a plan? Do you strongly support, somewhat support, somewhat oppose or strongly oppose it?" Princeton Survey Research Associates for the Evan B. Donaldson Institute, July 7-August 8, 1997.

CHAPTER 4 The Care of Children

101 Bureau of Labor Statistics, "Employment Status of the Population by Sex, Marital Status, and Presence and Age of Own Children Under 18, 2001-02 Annual Averages," Table 5, Available at *www.bls.gov/news.release/famee.t05.htm*. Percent calculations by the author.

102 Barbara Downs, *Fertility of American Women: June 2002*, Current Population Reports P20-548, U.S. Census Bureau, October 2003, Figure 3.

103 Ibid, Figure 2.

104 Kristin Smith, *Who's Minding the Kids? Child Care Arrangements: Fall 1997*, Current Population Reports, P70-86, U.S. Census Bureau, July 2002, Table 2. Percent calculations by the author.

105 Cheryl Wetzstein, "More Kids Cared for by Moms at Home," *The Washington Times*, June 17, 2003, p. A1.

106 U.S. Census Bureau, *Who's Minding the Kids? Child Care Arrangements: Spring 1999*, Historical Table, "Primary Child Care Arrangements Used by Employed Mothers of Preschoolers: 1985 to 1999."

107 U.S. Census Bureau, "Primary Child Care Arrangements Use for Preschoolers by Families with Employed Mothers: Selected Years, 1997 to 1994," January 14, 1998, Table A, Available at *www.census.gov/population/socdemo/child/p70-62/tableA.txt* and U.S. Census Bureau, *Who's Minding the Kids? Child Care Arrangements: Spring 1999*, Historical Table.

108 NICHD study, "Does Amount of Time Spent in Child Care Predict Socioemotional Adjustment During the Transition to Kindergarten?" *Child Development* 74 (2003): 976-1005.

109 Deborah L. Vandell, "Early Child Care and Children's Development Prior to School Entry," NICHD Early Child Care Research Network, National Institutes of Health, 2001.

110 John E. Bates, et al., "Child-Care History and Kindergarten Adjustment," *Developmental Psychology* 30 (1994): 690-700.

111 Elizabeth Harvey, "Short-Term and Long-Term Effects of Early Parental Employment on Children of the National Longitudinal Survey of Youth," *Developmental Psychology* 35 (1999): 445-459.

112 Lisabeth F. DiLalla, "Daycare, Child and Family Influences on Preschoolers' Social Behaviors in a Peer Play Setting," *Child Study Journal* 28 (1998): 223-244.

113 Jeanne Brooks-Gunn, et al., "Maternal Employment and Child Cognitive Outcomes in the First Three Years of Life: The NICHD Study of Early Child Care," *Child Development* 73 (July/August 2002): 1052-1072.

114 NICHD Early Child Care Research Network, "Child Care and Mother-Child Interaction in the First 3 Years of Life," *Developmental Psychology* 35 (1999): 1399-1413.

115 NICHD Early Child Care Research Network, "The Effects of Infant Child Care on Infant-Mother Attachment Security: Results of the NICHD Study of Early Child Care," *Child Development* 68 (1997): 860-879.

116 Orin S. Levine, et al., "Risk Factors for Invasive Pneumococcal Disease in Children: A Population-Based Case-Control Study in North America," *Pediatrics* 103 (March 1999).

117 James D. Kellner and E. Lee Ford-Jones, "Streptococcus pneumoniae Carriage in Children Attending 59 Canadian Child Care Centers," *Archives of Pediatrics & Adolescent Medicine* 153 (May 1999): 495-502.

118 Sarah E. Watamura, et al., "Morning-to-Afternoon Increases in Cortisol Concentrations for Infants and Toddlers at Child Care: Age Differences and Behavioral Correlates," *Child Development* 74 (July/August 2003): 1006-1020.

119 Per Nafstad, et al., "Day Care Centers and Respiratory Health," *Pediatrics* 103 (April 1999): 753-758.

120 Michael Silverstein, et al., "Health Care Utilization and Expenditures Associated with Child Care Attendance: A Nationally Representative Sample," *Pediatrics* 111 (April 2003): 371-375.

121 Wirthlin Worldwide for Family Research Council, "American's Attitudes Toward Child Care," Family Research Council, January, 1998.

122 Gallup Poll, April 20-22, 2001, Available at *www.gallup.com/poll/releases/pr010504.asp*.

123 Public Agenda, "Necessary Compromises," June 1-15, 2000. Responses are from parents with children age five or under.

124 CBS News, *New York Times* Poll, July 13-27, 2003.

125 Public Agenda, "Necessary Compromises."

126 Ibid.

127 Ibid.

128 Full question reads: "(As you know, over the past thirty years there have been many changes in the roles of women and men in our society. I'm going to describe some of those changes and for each one please tell me whether this is an area in which the country has not gone far enough, has gone too far, or has gone just far enough.)... Young children are spending more time with babysitters or in child care." Peter D. Hart Research Associates for Shell Oil Company, January 7-13, 2000.

129 The Pew Research Center, "Motherhood Today – A Tougher Job, Less Ably Done," May 1997.

130 Ibid.

131 Public Agenda, "Necessary Compromises."

132 CBS New Poll, July 13-14, 1999.

133 Public Agenda, "Necessary Compromises."

134 Ibid.

CHAPTER 5

Adult Unwed Sex & Adultery

The monstrosity of sexual intercourse outside marriage is that those who indulge in it are trying to isolate one kind of union (the sexual) from all the other kinds of union which were intended to go along with it and make up the total union.

—C. S. Lewis
Mere Christianity

BY THE NUMBERS: ADULT UNWED SEX

SNAPSHOT 1
Premarital sex is very common among younger women.

- In 1992, women age 18-29 were much more likely to have had premarital sex than were women age 50-59.

Percent of Women Who Have Not Had Premarital Sex, 1992

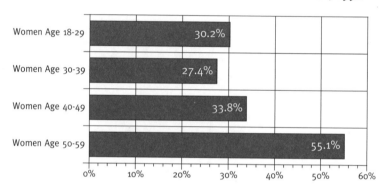

Women Age 18-29	30.2%
Women Age 30-39	27.4%
Women Age 40-49	33.8%
Women Age 50-59	55.1%

0% 10% 20% 30% 40% 50% 60%

YEAR OF BIRTH	PERCENT WHO HAVE NOT HAD PREMARITAL SEX	
	MEN	WOMEN
1933-1942	26.4%	55.1%
1943-1952	19.0%	33.8%
1953-1962	18.6%	27.4%
1963-1974	22.0%	30.2%

Source: The Social Organization of Sexuality [1]

SNAPSHOT 2
Most first-time sexual intercourse is voluntary.

- In 1992, 92.1 percent of men and 71.3 percent of women said their first experience of sexual intercourse was voluntary.

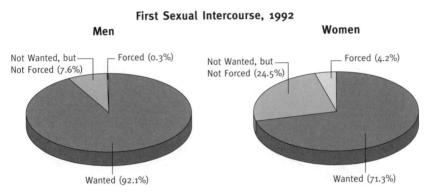

First Sexual Intercourse, 1992

Men

Not Wanted, but Not Forced (7.6%) — Forced (0.3%)

Wanted (92.1%)

Women

Not Wanted, but Not Forced (24.5%) — Forced (4.2%)

Wanted (71.3%)

Source: The Social Organization of Sexuality [2]

SNAPSHOT 3
Most married couples are sexually faithful.

- In 1992, 25 percent of men and 15 percent of women reported that they had committed adultery.[3]

YEAR OF BIRTH	PERCENT OF MEN WHO REPORTED COMMITTING ADULTERY	PERCENT OF WOMEN WHO REPORTED COMMITTING ADULTERY
1933-42	37.0%	12.4%
1943-52	31.4%	19.9%
1953-62	20.5%	14.5%
1963-74	7.1%	11.7%
All Years, 1933-74	24.5%	15.0%

Source: The Social Organization of Sexuality [4]

THE CONSEQUENCES OF ADULT UNWED SEX

Snapshot 1

Adults who engage in sex outside marriage express less sexual satisfaction than do married couples.

- Married people express greater physical pleasure and emotional satisfaction from sex than do unmarried people.

Percent Physically and Emotionally Satisfied by Sexual Relationship

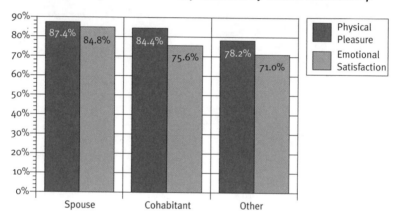

Source: The Social Organization of Sexuality [5]

- When asked how sex made them feel, cohabitants and other unmarried people were more likely than married men and women to say that it made them feel anxious, worried, afraid or guilty.

Percent Who Express Negative Emotions about Sex

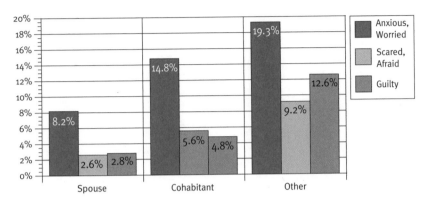

Source: *The Social Organization of Sexuality* [6]

SNAPSHOT 2
Premarital and extramarital sex weaken marriages.

- A 2002 study based on the National Survey of Family Growth reveals that women who have premarital sex, bear children out-of-wedlock, or premaritally cohabit are more likely to experience marital breakup.[7]

- A 2003 study of national data on people's reasons for divorcing found that infidelity was the most commonly reported cause.[8]

SNAPSHOT 3
Sex with multiple partners increases the risk of contracting sexually transmitted diseases (STDs), which result in costly treatments.[9]

The United States has the highest STD rates of any country in the industrialized world.

—The Kaiser Family Foundation[10]

- At least a third of sexually active people are estimated to have contracted an STD by age 24.[11]

- Two-thirds of all new STD infections occur among young people under age 25; forty-two percent occur among 20- to 24-year-olds and 25 percent occur among teens age 15-19.[12]

- Each year there are 15 million new cases of sexually transmitted diseases in the U.S., of which 50 percent are incurable.[13] More than 65 million people in the U.S. currently have an incurable STD.[14]

- Each year, a third of new STD cases are caused by human papillomavirus (HPV). Approximately 5.5 million people are infected with HPV annually and about 20 million people have the virus today, making it the most common STD.[15] HPV is an incurable virus that can cause genital warts and cervical cancer. Studies have shown that HPV is present in nearly all (99.7 percent) cervical cancers.[16]

- In 2000, the total direct medical cost for diagnosing and treating nine million new cases of STDs among young people age 15-24 was $6.5 billion, with HIV and HPV accounting for 90 percent of the total cost.[17]

SNAPSHOT 4
Most abortions occur after unwed sex.

- Approximately 83 percent of abortions are obtained by unmarried women; two-thirds are obtained by never-married women.[18]

WHAT THE POLLS SAY ABOUT ADULT UNWED SEX

SNAPSHOT 1
Most Americans do not think it is wrong for a man and a woman to engage in sex outside marriage.

- In a 2003 poll, 58 percent of adults said sex between an unmarried man and woman is morally acceptable.

Question: "Regardless of whether or not you think it should be legal ... please tell me whether you personally believe that in general it is morally acceptable or morally wrong ... sex between an unmarried man and woman?"

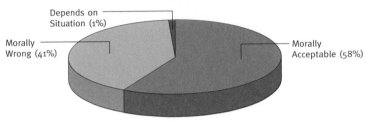

Depends on Situation (1%)

Morally Wrong (41%)

Morally Acceptable (58%)

Source: Gallup Poll [19]

SNAPSHOT 2
Most Americans think adultery is always wrong.

- In 2002, 79 percent of adults said adultery is always wrong.

Question: "What is your opinion about a married person having sexual relations with someone other than the marriage partner—is it always wrong, almost always wrong, wrong only sometimes, or not wrong at all?"

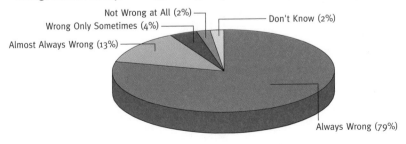

Not Wrong at All (2%)

Don't Know (2%)

Wrong Only Sometimes (4%)

Almost Always Wrong (13%)

Always Wrong (79%)

Source: General Social Survey [20]

- In 2003, 93 percent of adults said adultery is morally wrong.

Question: "Regardless of whether or not you think it should be legal . . . please tell whether you personally believe that in general it is morally acceptable or morally wrong . . . Married men and women having an affair."

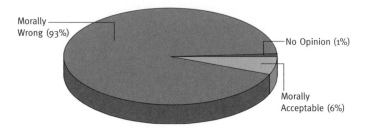

Source: Gallup Poll [21]

CHAPTER 6

Adult Unwed Childbearing

Men and women come to feel we have a right—a natural right—to sex without pregnancy. We feel our bodies are betraying us when sex leads to babies.

—Maggie Gallagher
Enemies of Eros

BY THE NUMBERS: ADULT UNWED CHILDBEARING

SNAPSHOT 1
In 2002, one of every three babies was born outside marriage.

- In 2002, the number of births to unmarried women reached 1,365,966, the highest number reported to date.[22]

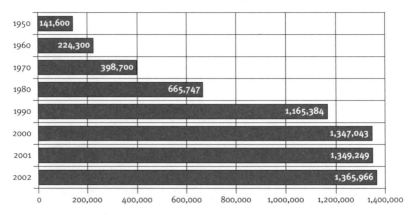

Number of Unwed Births, Historical

Year	Number
1950	141,600
1960	224,300
1970	398,700
1980	665,747
1990	1,165,384
2000	1,347,043
2001	1,349,249
2002	1,365,966

YEAR	NUMBER OF UNWED BIRTHS	PERCENTAGE OF ALL BIRTHS THAT WERE UNWED
1940	89,500	3.8%
1945	117,400	4.3%
1950	141,600	4.0%
1955	183,300	4.5%
1960	224,300	5.3%
1965	291,200	7.7%
1970	398,700	10.7%
1975	447,900	14.3%
1980	665,747	18.4%
1985	828,174	22.0%
1990	1,165,384	28.0%
1995	1,253,976	32.2%
1996	1,260,306	32.4%
1997	1,257,444	32.4%
1998	1,293,567	32.8%
1999	1,308,560	33.0%
2000	1,347,043	33.2%
2001	1,349,249	33.5%
2002	1,365,966	34.0%

Source: National Center for Health Statistics [23]

SNAPSHOT 2

The number of children born outside marriage has risen sharply since the 1930s.

- From 1930 to 1934, one in six first births to women age 15-29 was either conceived or born before marriage. By 1990-1994, this figure had increased to one in two births.[24]

- Between 1990 and 1994, 41 percent of first births among 15- to 29-year-old women occurred outside of marriage, compared to just eight percent from 1950 to 1954.

Percentage of First Births that Were Premarital among Women Age 15-29, Historical

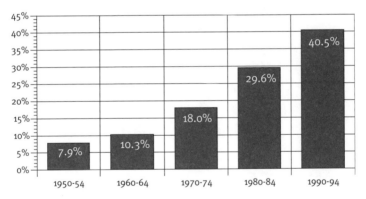

Source: U.S. Census Bureau [25]

- Between 1960 and 1964, 74 percent of first births among women age 15-29 were conceived after marriage, compared to 47 percent between 1990 and 1994.

Births among Women Age 15-29, Historical

Year	Total Number of First Births Among Women Age 15-29	Percent of First Births that Were Premarital	Percent of First Births that Were Conceived Outside Marriage	Percent of First Births that Were Conceived After Marriage
1930-34	2,279,000	8.2%	9.5%	82.2%
1935-39	3,036,000	8.5%	9.0%	82.6%
1940-44	3,982,000	7.0%	7.5%	85.5%
1945-49	4,971,000	7.6%	7.9%	84.6%
1950-54	5,004,000	7.9%	9.3%	82.8%
1955-59	5,173,000	10.0%	10.9%	79.1%
1960-64	5,507,000	10.3%	15.5%	74.3%
1965-69	5,929,000	15.1%	18.0%	66.9%
1970-74	6,438,000	18.0%	17.1%	64.8%
1975-79	6,626,000	25.7%	12.0%	62.2%
1980-84	6,842,000	29.6%	12.3%	58.1%
1985-89	6,364,000	32.7%	10.7%	56.5%
1990-94	6,324,000	40.5%	12.3%	47.2%

Source: U.S. Census Bureau [26]

- Between 1960 and 1964, 60 percent of unwed pregnant women age 15-29 married before the birth of their children, compared to 23 percent in the early 1990s.[27]

- In 2002, over one-fifth of never-married women age 15-44 were mothers.[28]

Snapshot 3
The annual birthrate has decreased among married women and increased among unmarried women over the past fifty years.

- From 1960 to 2002, the birthrate among unmarried women more than doubled, while the birthrate among married women fell by 45 percent.

Birthrates among Married and Unmarried Women, Historical

Annual Number of Births per 1,000 **Married** Women Age 15-44

Annual Number of Births per 1,000 **Unmarried** Women Age 15-44

Source: National Center for Health Statistics [29]

SNAPSHOT 4
The percentage of out-of-wedlock births among black women has decreased since 1994.

- Among black women, the percentage of births outside marriage has decreased from 70.4 percent in 1994 to 68.2 percent in 2002. Among Hispanic women, the percentage of unwed births declined slightly after 1994 but has increased since 1997.

- Among white women, the percentage of births outside marriage steadily increased during the 1990s.

Percent of Births among Women Age 15 and Older that were Out of Wedlock, 1990-2002

Year	Percent of Unwed Births Among White Women	Percent of Unwed Births Among Black Women	Percent of Unwed Births Among Hispanic Women
1990	20.4%	66.5%	36.7%
1991	21.8%	67.9%	38.5%
1992	22.6%	68.1%	39.1%
1993	23.6%	68.7%	40.0%
1994	25.4%	70.4%	43.1%
1995	25.3%	69.9%	40.8%
1996	25.7%	69.8%	40.7%
1997	25.8%	69.2%	40.9%
1998	26.3%	69.1%	41.6%
1999	26.7%	68.8%	42.1%
2000	27.1%	68.5%	42.7%
2001	27.7%	68.4%	42.5%
2002	28.5%	68.2%	43.5%

Source: National Center for Health Statistics [30]

- In 2002, 29 percent of white births, 68 percent of black births and 44 percent of Hispanic births were out of wedlock.

Percent of Births that Were Out of Wedlock, by Race, 2002

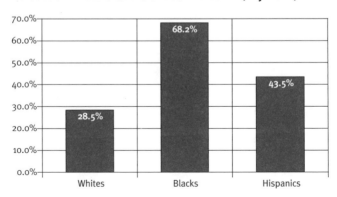

SNAPSHOT 5
The unwed birthrate is higher among women in their twenties than among teens.

- In 2002, the unwed birthrate was highest among women age 20-24.

Birthrates for Unmarried Women, by Age, 1960 and 2002

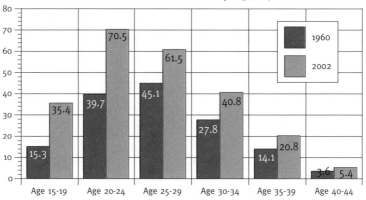

Birthrates for Unmarried Women, by Age, Historical

YEAR	ALL WOMEN, AGE 15-44	AGE 15-19	AGE 20-24	AGE 25-29	AGE 30-34	AGE 35-39	AGE 40-44
1940	7.1	7.4	9.5	7.2	5.1	3.4	1.2
1950	14.1	12.6	21.3	19.9	13.3	7.2	2.0
1955	19.3	15.1	33.5	33.5	22.0	10.5	2.7
1960	21.6	15.3	39.7	45.1	27.8	14.1	3.6
1965	23.4	16.7	39.6	49.1	37.2	17.4	4.5
1970	26.4	22.4	38.4	37.0	27.1	13.6	3.5
1975	24.5	23.9	31.2	27.5	17.9	9.1	2.6
1980	29.4	27.6	40.9	34.0	21.1	9.7	2.6
1985	32.8	31.4	46.5	39.9	25.2	11.6	2.5
1990	43.8	42.5	65.1	56.0	37.6	17.3	3.6
1993	44.8	44.0	68.3	55.9	38.0	18.9	4.4
1995	44.3	43.8	68.7	54.3	38.9	19.3	4.7
2000	44.0	39.0	72.1	58.5	39.3	19.7	5.0
2002	43.7	35.4	70.5	61.5	40.8	20.8	5.4

Note: Birthrate is the annual number of births per 1,000 unmarried women.

Source: National Center for Health Statistics [31]

SNAPSHOT 6
In 2002, the District of Columbia had the highest percentage of out-of-wedlock births in the U.S., while Utah had the lowest.

Percent of Out-of-Wedlock Births, 2002

STATE	PERCENT OF BIRTHS THAT WERE OUT OF WEDLOCK, 2002	STATE	PERCENT OF BIRTHS THAT WERE OUT OF WEDLOCK, 2002
United States	34.0%	Maine	32.6%
District of Columbia	56.5%	Texas	32.4%
Mississippi	47.1%	Vermont	31.9%
Louisiana	47.0%	Kansas	31.1%
New Mexico	46.9%	Oregon	30.9%
Delaware	40.6%	Virginia	30.3%
Arizona	40.4%	Wyoming	30.3%
South Carolina	40.4%	Wisconsin	30.0%
Florida	39.3%	Iowa	29.3%
Georgia	37.8%	New Jersey	29.3%
Nevada	37.4%	Connecticut	29.1%
Arkansas	37.1%	North Dakota	29.0%
Indiana	36.4%	Washington	28.8%
Oklahoma	36.4%	Nebraska	28.6%
Tennessee	36.2%	Minnesota	27.4%
New York	35.7%	Colorado	26.8%
Rhode Island	35.7%	Massachusetts	26.8%
Ohio	35.4%	New Hampshire	24.6%
Missouri	35.2%	Idaho	21.9%
South Dakota	35.0%	Utah	17.2%
Alabama	34.8%		
Illinois	34.8%		
Maryland	34.8%		
North Carolina	34.7%		
Michigan	34.1%		
Alaska	34.0%		
Hawaii	33.6%		
Pennsylvania	33.4%		
Kentucky	33.2%		
California	33.0%		
West Virginia	32.9%		
Montana	32.8%		

Source: National Center for Health Statistics [32]

THE CONSEQUENCES OF ADULT UNWED CHILDBEARING

SNAPSHOT 1
Children born outside marriage are likely to grow up without married parents.

- According to demographer Larry Bumpass, one-third of the first-born children of unmarried women will spend all of their childhood without married parents. One-fifth of white children and three-fifths of black children will live in a family without married parents during childhood.[33]

- A 2001 study found that couples who had a child before they entered marriage were twice as likely to divorce than were couples who did not enter marriage with children.[34]

SNAPSHOT 2
Unwed childbearing leaves parents and children economically disadvantaged.

- A 1999 study found that women who have children out of wedlock are likely to have a much lower income than are married women; they are six times more likely to be on welfare and 40 percent less likely to be working full time.[35]

- In a longitudinal study of 5,000 children and their unmarried parents, interviews revealed that nearly 30 percent of fathers were out of work the week before they were surveyed. Thirty-seven percent of the mothers and 34 percent of the fathers did not have a high school degree.[36]

- According to a 2003 study, women who have a child out of wedlock as a teen or as an adult are four times more likely to be poor than are other women.[37]

Snapshot 3
Unwed mothers and fathers are less likely to marry.

- A 2002 study found that unwed mothers are less likely to marry than are women who do not have children outside of marriage. For example, 82 percent of white women, 62 percent of Hispanic women and 59 percent of blacks whose first births were out of wedlock married by age 40; for those who married and did not have a child out of wedlock, the respective figures were 89 percent of white women, 93 percent of Hispanics and 76 percent of blacks.[38]

- A 2003 study of national data found that women who had their first child within marriage were twice as likely to be currently married than were women who had their first child out of wedlock (82 percent vs. 41 percent).[39]

- A 1998 study found that young men who father a child outside marriage are much less likely to marry and twice as likely to cohabit than are those who do not.[40]

Snapshot 4
Men and women who have children out of wedlock are likely to suffer from depression.

- A 2003 national study of over 1,900 adults found that never-married men and women who became parents and did not marry had a much higher incidence of depression than did adults who had their first child in marriage. Never-married fathers had the highest incidence of depression, which, according to the researchers, may be due to their lack of contact with their new child.[41]

WHAT THE POLLS SAY ABOUT ADULT UNWED CHILDBEARING

SNAPSHOT 1
Most Americans believe it is best for a child to be born to married parents.

- More than 80 percent of Americans believe that marriage is a prerequisite to having children, according to a 1999 survey.

Question: "Do you agree or disagree ... People who want children ought to get married?"

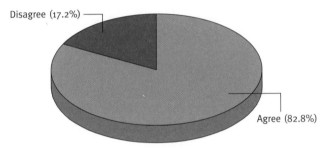

Disagree (17.2%)

Agree (82.8%)

Source: General Social Survey [42]

SNAPSHOT 2
Half of all Americans believe out-of-wedlock childbearing is morally acceptable.

- In 2003, 51 percent of those surveyed said having a baby outside of marriage is morally acceptable.

Question: "Regardless of whether or not you think it should be legal...
please tell me whether you personally believe that in general it is
morally acceptable or morally wrong. How about...having a baby
outside of marriage?"

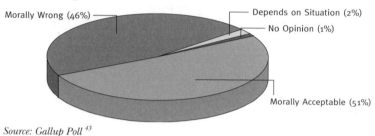

Morally Wrong (46%)

Depends on Situation (2%)

No Opinion (1%)

Morally Acceptable (51%)

Source: Gallup Poll [43]

SNAPSHOT 3

Americans who attend weekly church services are the least likely
to approve of out-of-wedlock childbearing.

- In a 2003 poll, only 26 percent of weekly churchgoers said
  having a baby outside marriage is morally acceptable, compared to 71 percent of those who seldom or never attend
  church.

Question: "Regardless of whether or not you think it should be legal
...please tell me whether you personally believe that in general it is
morally acceptable or morally wrong. How about...having a baby
outside of marriage?"

Percent Saying "Morally Acceptable"

Attend Church Weekly	Attend Church Nearly Weekly	Seldom or Never Attend
26%	53%	71%

Source: Gallup Poll [44]

SNAPSHOT 4

Married people are less likely to approve of out-of-wedlock child-bearing than are unmarried adults.

- In a 2003 poll, 45 percent of married people said out-of-wed-lock childbearing was acceptable, compared to 58 percent of the unmarried.

Question: "Regardless of whether or not you think it should be legal . . . please tell me whether you personally believe that in general it is morally acceptable or morally wrong. How about . . . having a baby outside of marriage?"

Percent Saying "Morally Acceptable"

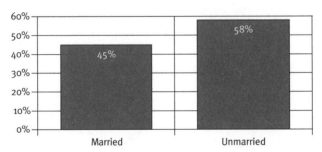

Source: *Gallup Poll* [45]

CHAPTER 7

Cohabitation

Widespread cohabitation delivers, in practice, nothing of what it promises in theory. To the contrary, it undermines lasting attachments, mutual obligations, successful child-rearing, and sexual fidelity. It undermines those precious things themselves, and it undermines our belief in them. What it offers instead is kind of institutionalized adolescence: a dream of free love freely bestowed, a love relying solely on the springs of mutual emotion and independent of the legal and other constraints imposed by state and society and their surrogates in the form of traditional family arrangements.

—William J. Bennett
*The Broken Hearth: Reversing the Moral
Collapse of the American Family*

BY THE NUMBERS: COHABITATION

Snapshot 1
The number of cohabiting couples has increased dramatically in recent decades.

- In 1970, just over a half a million couples cohabited; by 2002, 4.9 million unmarried couples were living together.

Number of Cohabiting Couples, 1960-2002

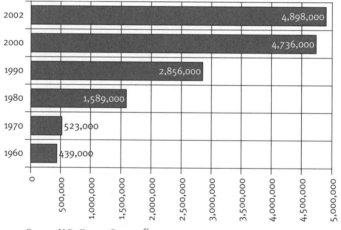

Year	Number
2002	4,898,000
2000	4,736,000
1990	2,856,000
1980	1,589,000
1970	523,000
1960	439,000

Source: U.S. Census Bureau [46]

Snapshot 2
More than half of all first marriages are preceded by cohabitation.[47]

- Between 1965 and 1974 only 10 percent of marriages were preceded by cohabitation, compared to 56 percent between 1990 and 1994.

Marriages Preceded by Cohabitation

1965-1974   **1990-1994**

10% of Marriages
Preceded by Cohabitation

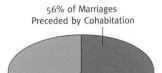
56% of Marriages
Preceded by Cohabitation

Source: Annual Review of Sociology, 2000 [48]

SNAPSHOT 3

Thirty years ago, most cohabiting couples were older than 45; today half are between 25 and 44.

- In 1970, 70 percent of cohabiting couples were age 45 and older; today one out of two are age 25-44.

Percent of Cohabiting Couples Age 25-44 and Age 45 and Older

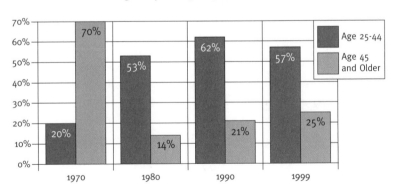

Source: U.S. Census Bureau [49]

SNAPSHOT 4
One-third of cohabiting households include children under age 15.

- In 2002, 34 percent of cohabiting couples lived with children under age 15.

Cohabiting Households with Children under 15, 1960-2002

YEAR	TOTAL NUMBER OF COHABITING COUPLES	PERCENT OF COHABITING COUPLES WITH CHILDREN UNDER AGE 15
1960	439,000	45%
1970	523,000	37%
1980	1,589,000	27%
1985	1,983,000	30%
1990	2,856,000	31%
1995	3,668,000	36%
2000	4,736,000	35%
2002	4,898,000	34%

Source: U.S. Census Bureau [50]

- In 2000, four out of ten cohabiting households had children under age 18.[51]

- Almost 50 percent of cohabiting couples age 25-34 have children in their households.[52]

- In the 1990s, 40 percent of out-of-wedlock births occurred in cohabiting unions.[53]

- About 65 percent of Hispanic children born outside marriage have cohabiting parents, compared to 57 percent of white children and 26 percent of black children.[54]

SNAPSHOT 5
Cohabiting relationships are likely to be unstable and to lead to future marital breakup.

- Only 46 percent of cohabiting relationships are considered "precursors to marriage," meaning those in which couples have definite plans to marry each other. The rest are trial marriages (15 percent), coresidential dating (29 percent), and substitutes for marriage (10 percent). Researchers found that after 5-7 years, only 40 percent of all cohabiting couples had married, while 39 percent had separated and 21 percent still lived together.[55]

- The probability of a woman's first cohabiting relationship terminating is 39 percent after three years, 49 percent after five years, and 62 percent after 10 years.[56]

- Couples who premaritally cohabit have a 40 percent chance of marital breakup after ten years, compared to 31 percent for those who do not live together before marriage.[57]

- In a 2003 study, married couples who lived together before marriage had a 65 percent "greater risk of dissolution" than did couples who did not live together before marriage.[58]

THE CONSEQUENCES OF COHABITATION: A COMPARISON OF MARRIAGE AND COHABITATION

SNAPSHOT 1
Cohabitants are less healthy emotionally than are married couples.

- The instability of cohabiting relationships contributes to more frequent depression among cohabitants, according to a study published in 2000. Cohabitants in long, unstable unions have depression levels that are one-third higher than those of married people. Cohabitants who live with biological children or stepchildren are depressed more frequently than are married couples with children.[59]

- A 1995 study based on national data found that cohabiting couples reported less commitment and happiness and poorer relationships with their parents than did married couples.[60]

- A 1998 17-nation study found that married men and women report higher levels of happiness than do cohabiting couples.[61]

SNAPSHOT 2
Cohabitation is not as safe as marriage.

- In a 2002 study, cohabiting couples reported rates of physical aggression in their relationships that were three times higher than those reported by married couples.[62]

- A 2001 study found that, compared to married women, cohabiting women are about 9 times more likely to be murdered by their partner.[63]

- A 2003 study of over 4,000 couples found that, compared to married women, cohabiting women are at much higher risk for experiencing "intense male violence."[64]

SNAPSHOT 3
Cohabitants are less happy and less faithful to their relationships than are married couples.

- A 2002 study of 5,642 adults found that, compared to married and remarried couples, long-term cohabiting couples are the least happy with their relationships and the least satisfied with the amount of love and understanding they receive from each other. Also, long-term cohabiting couples scored the lowest on perceived levels of fairness with regard to working for pay, spending money and doing household chores.[65]

- A 2003 study of 3,732 adults found that, compared to married couples, cohabitants are less happy with their relationships and report more instability. Long-term cohabiting couples report particularly high levels of instability and low levels of happiness.[66]

- Cohabitants are twice as likely to be unfaithful as are married people, according to a 2000 study. Even when researchers controlled for their more permissive attitudes about extramarital sex, cohabitants showed greater infidelity, leading researchers to conclude that their "lower investments" in cohabiting unions—rather than their values—accounted for the increased infidelity.[67]

Cohabitants tend not to be as committed as married couples in their dedication to the continuation of the relationship and reluctance to terminate it, and they are more oriented toward their own personal autonomy. . . . Once this low-commitment, high-autonomy pattern of relating is learned, it becomes hard to unlearn.

—David Popenoe and Barbara Dafoe Whitehead
*Should We Live Together? What Young Adults
Need to Know about Cohabitation before Marriage*

SNAPSHOT 4
Cohabiting households are more likely to be poor than are married-couple families.

- A 2002 study of national data on parents with children under 18 found that the poverty rate of cohabiting couples is twice that of married parents. According to the study, cohabiting couples with children experience more material hardship than do married parents, because they have less access to help from family, friends and community resources.[68]

- Cohabiting couples with children have lower levels of education and income than do married parents.[69]

- Cohabiting families are less likely than intact families to inherit wealth from their extended families.[70]

SNAPSHOT 5
Cohabitants are less religiously active than are married couples.

- Cohabitants are typically less religious than their peers, according to the National Marriage Project.[71]

- A 1992 study found that cohabitation has a negative effect on young people's religious participation, while marriage has a positive effect. Young people who presently or previously cohabited attended fewer religious services after entering a cohabiting union. Those who married without first cohabiting increased their religious attendance after marriage.[72]

THE EFFECTS OF COHABITATION ON MARRIAGE

SNAPSHOT 1
Cohabitants are at high risk for later divorce.

- In a 2003 study, married couples who lived together before marriage had a 65 percent greater "risk of dissolution" than did couples who did not live together before marriage.[73]

- A 1995 Canadian study found that couples who premaritally cohabited are at much higher risk for divorce, even after adjusting for the presence of stepchildren, differences in spouses' ages, prior marital status and parental divorce.[74]

SNAPSHOT 2
Cohabitants often experience poorer communication and greater conflict in marriage than do married couples.

- A 2002 study determined that married couples who cohabit before marriage have poorer communication skills than do non-cohabiting couples. The authors of the study suggested that poor communication may contribute to the high marital breakup rate among couples who live together before marriage.[75]

- A 2003 study of 1,425 spouses found that, compared to those who did not live together before marriage, those who premaritally cohabited experienced less marital happiness; reported more disagreements, serious quarrels and aggression; and were twice as likely to divorce.[76]

SNAPSHOT 3
Cohabitants are likely to lack a commitment to marriage and family.

- A 1997 study found that young adults who cohabited ·between age 18 and 23 developed negative attitudes toward marriage, found divorce more acceptable and desired fewer children than did non-cohabiting couples. The authors of the study noted that "the more months of exposure to cohabitation that young people experienced, the less enthusiastic they were toward marriage and childbearing."[77]

- A 2000 study found that couples who cohabit prior to marriage are 39 percent more likely to experience marital infidelity than are couples who do not live together before marriage.[78]

THE EFFECTS OF COHABITATION ON CHILDREN

According to demographer Larry Bumpass, two out of five children will spend some time in a cohabiting household before age 16.[79]

SNAPSHOT 1
Children living in cohabiting households are likely to experience family breakup.

- Before reaching age 16, three-quarters of children born to cohabiting couples will experience the breakup of their parents' relationship; only one-third of children born to married parents will experience parental divorce or separation.[80]

- According to a study of 1,409 fathers who were living with their child's mother at the time of their child's birth, cohabiting men were more than twice as likely as married men to move away from their children during a 30-year period.[81]

SNAPSHOT 2
Children in cohabiting households are likely to have emotional and behavioral problems.

- Compared to children raised by their married biological parents, more children in cohabiting households experience emotional and behavioral problems, such as difficultly getting along with peers, difficulty in concentrating as well as feelings of sadness or depression. Among adolescents age 12-17, the percentage of those exhibiting emotional and behavioral problems was six times greater in cohabiting stepfamilies than in married biological-parent families.[82]

- A 2002 study conducted by The Urban Institute found that, compared to children raised by their married biological parents, children living in cohabiting households are more than twice as likely to be poor and to have emotional and behavioral problems. Also, children in cohabiting households are less likely to be read to, and their parents are twice as likely to have difficulty providing sufficient food.[83]

SNAPSHOT 3
Children in cohabiting households experience greater educational difficulties.

- Children in cohabiting households are less inclined to care about school and homework performance,[84] and their academic performance is poorer than that of children living with their married biological parents.[85]

- A 2001 study found that white and Hispanic teenagers in cohabiting households were more likely to be suspended or expelled from school and to be less motivated to do schoolwork than were teens living with single parents or married biological parents.[86]

- Compared to teens raised by their married biological parents, teens living with their mother and her cohabiting partner are 122 percent more likely to be expelled from school and 90 percent more likely to have a low grade point average, according to a 2003 study of over 13,000 adolescents. Teens raised in cohabiting households are also more likely to be delinquent. They are also more likely to have problems at school, such as getting along with students and teachers, paying attention in class and completing homework assignments.[87]

SNAPSHOT 4
Children in cohabiting households are more likely to be economically disadvantaged.

- A 1996 study found that children in cohabiting households are much more likely to live in poverty than are children with married parents. The authors of the study suggest that children with married parents fare better economically because their parents have more education and income.[88]

- Compared to children with married parents, four times as many children in cohabiting homes live in poverty.[89]

- A 2002 study of national data on parents with children under 18 found that the poverty rate of cohabiting couples is twice that of married parents. According to the study, cohabiting couples with children experience more material hardship than do married parents, because they have less access to help from family, friends and community resources.[90]

WHAT THE POLLS SAY ABOUT COHABITATION

SNAPSHOT 1
More than half of Americans approve of cohabitation.

- A 2000 poll found that 56 percent of respondents find it acceptable for an engaged couple to live together before marriage.

Question: "Would you say it is acceptable or unacceptable for an engaged couple to live together prior to marriage?"

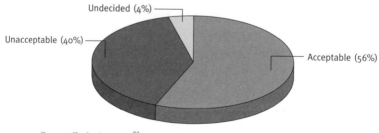

Undecided (4%)

Unacceptable (40%)

Acceptable (56%)

Source: Zogby America [91]

- A 2001 poll found that 52 percent say it is morally acceptable to cohabit.

Question: "Do you personally think that it is morally acceptable or morally unacceptable for an unmarried man and woman to live together?"

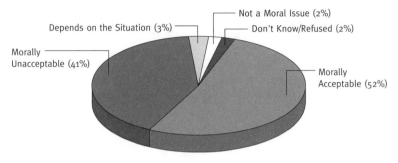

Source: Gallup, CNN, USA Today [92]

- In 2002, 48 percent of adults agreed that it's a good idea for couples intending to marry to live together before marriage.

Question: "To what extent do you agree or disagree ... It's a good idea for a couple who intend to get married to live together first?"

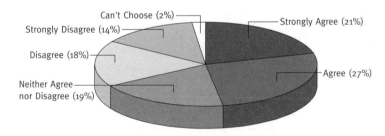

Source: General Social Survey [93]

SNAPSHOT 2
The majority of young people approve of cohabitation.

- Over the past 25 years, high school seniors have become more accepting of cohabitation.

Question: "How much do you agree or disagree with the following statement? It is usually a good idea for a couple to live together before getting married in order to find out whether they really get along."

Percent Who Support Cohabitation before Marriage

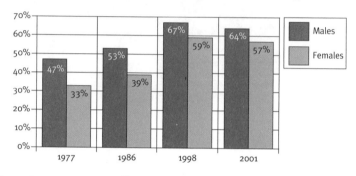

Source: Monitoring the Future [94]

• In a 2002 survey, only 19 percent of high school seniors expressed negative views on cohabitation. Eighty-two percent said cohabiting couples are "experimenting with a worthwhile alternative lifestyle" or "doing their own thing and not affecting anyone else."

Question: "A man and a woman who live together without being married are . . . "

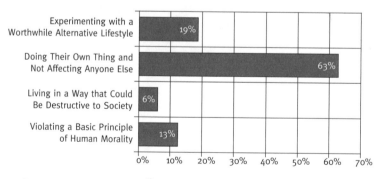

Source: Monitoring the Future [95]

CHAPTER 8

Divorce

Not so long ago marriage was an economic bond of mutual dependency, a social bond heavily upheld by extended families, and a religious bond of sacramental worth. Today, marriage is none of these. . . . Marriage has become a purely individual pursuit; an implied and not very enforceable contract between two people; a relationship designed to satisfy basic needs for intimacy, dependency and sex. When these needs change, or when a presumptively better partner is discovered, marriages are easily dissolved.

—David Popenoe
"Can the Nuclear Family Be Revived?"
Society, July-August 1999

BY THE NUMBERS: DIVORCE

SNAPSHOT 1

The annual divorce rate has almost doubled since 1960, but has declined since the 1980's.

- In 2001, the divorce rate among married women age 15 and older was 17.8 divorces per thousand married women, almost double the divorce rate in 1960.

- Based on projections of current divorce rates, between 40 and 50 percent of marriages today are likely to end in divorce or separation before one partner dies. Compared to first marriages, second and subsequent marriages have a somewhat higher chance of break up, due to their higher divorce rates.[96]

Marriage and Divorce Rates, Historical

YEAR	NUMBER OF DIVORCES	DIVORCE RATE
1940	264,000	8.8
1950	385,000	10.3
1955	377,000	9.3
1960	393,000	9.2
1965	479,000	10.6
1970	708,000	14.9
1975	1,036,000	20.3
1980	1,189,000	22.6
1985	1,190,000	21.7
1990	1,182,000	20.9
1991	1,189,000	20.9
1992	1,215,000	21.2
1993	1,187,000	20.5
1994	1,191,000	20.5
1995	1,169,000	19.8
1996	1,150,000	19.5
2000	N/A	18.8
2001	N/A	17.8

Divorce Rate among Married Women Age 15 and Older, 1960-2001

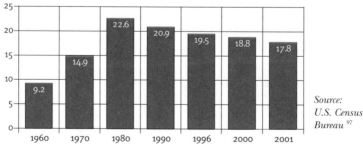

Source: U.S. Census Bureau [97]

Note: Divorce rate is the number of divorces per year per 1,000 married women, age 15 and older.

- While the annual divorce rate has increased since 1960, the annual marriage rate has decreased.

Marriage and Divorce Rates 1960-2001

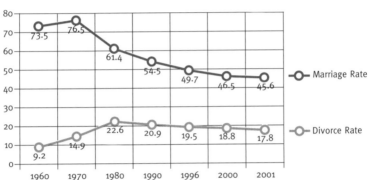

- The marriage rate among unmarried women age 15 and older decreased by nearly 50 percent between 1950 and 2001, while the annual divorce rate increased by 73 percent during these years.

Marriage and Divorce Rates, Historical

Year	Marriage Rate	Divorce Rate
1940	82.8	8.8
1950	90.2	10.3
1955	80.9	9.3
1960	73.5	9.2
1965	75.0	10.6
1970	76.5	14.9
1975	66.9	20.3
1980	61.4	22.6
1985	57.0	21.7
1990	54.5	20.9
1991	54.2	20.9
1992	53.3	21.2
1993	52.3	20.5
1994	51.5	20.5
1995	50.8	19.8
1996	49.7	19.5
2000	46.5	18.8
2001	45.6	17.8

Note: Marriage rate is the number of marriages per year per 1,000 unmarried women age 15 and older. Divorce rate is the number of divorces per year per 1,000 married women age 15 and older.

Source: U.S. Census Bureau [98]

SNAPSHOT 2
One-fifth of all adults have been divorced.

- In 1996, one-third of those age 40-59 had been divorced.

Percent of Adults Ever Divorced, 1996

AGE	PERCENT OF ADULTS EVER DIVORCED
25 – 29	9.8%
30 – 34	18.5%
35 – 39	26.1%
40 – 49	35.6%
50 – 59	35.2%
60 – 69	26.5%
70 and Older	17.4%
Total, 15 and Older	21.3%

Source: U.S. Census Bureau [99]

Today all of us are children of divorce, however happy our own or our parents' marriage. We have seen what happened to an aunt, a neighbor, a brother, or a friend. People are afraid to invest in a relationship in which they know from hard experience what the law teaches: The one who leaves, wins. The law now treats divorce as a private decision, the unilateral lifestyle preference of one partner.

—Maggie Gallagher
The Abolition of Marriage:
How We Destroy Lasting Love

SNAPSHOT 3
The advent of no-fault divorce in 1969 led to increased divorce.

- The enactment of no-fault divorce laws led to increases in divorce rates in 44 out of 50 states.[100]

- A 1998 study found that no-fault divorce laws caused a 17 percent increase in state-level divorce rates between 1968 and 1988.[101]

Snapshot 4
Nevada had the highest divorce rate among the states in 2001.

- In 2001, the average divorce rate in the 50 states and the District of Columbia was 4.0 divorces per thousand people.

State-by-State Divorce Rates, 2001

STATE	DIVORCE RATE	STATE	DIVORCE RATE
Nevada	6.8	South Carolina	3.5
Arkansas	6.6	Oklahoma	3.4
Wyoming	6.1	South Dakota	3.4
Idaho	5.6	Minnesota	3.3
Kentucky	5.5	Rhode Island	3.3
Colorado	5.5*	Illinois	3.2
Florida	5.4	Iowa	3.2
Mississippi	5.4	Kansas	3.2
Alabama	5.3	Pennsylvania	3.2
Tennessee	5.2	Wisconsin	3.2
West Virginia	5.2	Maryland	3.0
New Mexico	5.1	New York	3.0
New Hampshire	5.0	Connecticut	2.9
Oregon	4.9	North Dakota	2.7
North Carolina	4.5	Montana	2.6
Washington	4.5	Massachusetts	2.4
Utah	4.4	District of Columbia	2.3
Missouri	4.3	Indiana	N/A*
Virginia	4.3	Louisiana	N/A*
California	4.3		
Arizona	4.2		
Alaska	4.1		
Texas	4.1		
Delaware	4.0		
Ohio	4.0		
Vermont	4.0		
Maine	3.9		
Michigan	3.9		
Georgia	3.8		
Hawaii	3.8		
Nebraska	3.7		
New Jersey	3.5		

*Note: Divorce rate is the number of divorces per year per 1,000 people. *Colorado's divorce rate is based on 1994 data, and California's from 1990; this statistic is not available for Indiana or Louisiana since 1990.*

Source: U.S. Census Bureau [102]

SNAPSHOT 5

Since 1975, more than one million children have been affected by divorce each year.

- In 1990, the parents of more than one million children chose to divorce, more than double the number of children affected by divorce in 1960.

- Twenty-five percent of the adult population age 44 or younger have divorced parents.[103]

Number of Children Whose Parents Divorced, 1960-1990

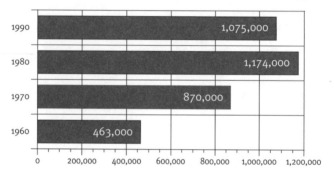

YEAR	NUMBER OF CHILDREN WHOSE PARENTS DIVORCED
1960	463,000
1965	630,000
1970	870,000
1975	1,123,000
1978	1,147,000
1980	1,174,000
1985	1,091,000
1990	1,075,000

Source: U.S. Census Bureau [104]

SNAPSHOT 6

Most divorces are initiated by women and occur in unhappy, rather than in high-conflict, marriages.

- The largest federally funded study on divorced fathers found that two-thirds of divorces are initiated by women.[105]

- A 15-year study found that less than one-third of divorces occur in high-conflict (e.g., abusive, violent) marriages; most occur in low-conflict but unhappy marriages.[106]

SNAPSHOT 7

The average length of a first marriage that ends in divorce is seven or eight years.[107]

- Ninety percent of women who were first married in 1945-1949 reached their 10th anniversary, and 81 percent reached their twentieth. Only 73 percent of those first married between 1980 and 1984 reached their 10th anniversary.[108]

- Twenty percent of first marriages end within five years and 33 percent end within 10 years.[109]

SNAPSHOT 8

Divorce burdens the American taxpayer.

- According to a 2003 study, divorce costs the United States $33.3 billion per year. This total includes direct costs to federal and state government for child support enforcement, Medicaid, Temporary Assistance to Needy Families, food stamps and public housing. Other indirect costs include those associated with unwed childbearing and the care of elderly singles, as well as the expenses incurred through drug use, delinquency, the maintenance of correctional facilities and other social problems related to divorce.[110]

- The "average" divorce costs state and federal governments $30,000 in direct and indirect costs.[111]

THE CONSEQUENCES OF DIVORCE: THE EFFECTS OF DIVORCE ON CHILDREN

SNAPSHOT 1

Children of divorced parents are more likely to have emotional, behavioral, and health problems than are children from intact families.

- In her extensive research on children of divorce, Judith Wallerstein found that following divorce, children experience feelings of rejection, loneliness, anger, guilt, anxiety, fear of abandonment by their parents and a deep yearning for the absent parent. Five years after their parents' divorce, 37 percent of the children Wallerstein studied were moderately or severely depressed.[112]

- A 1999 study found higher incidences of depression and delinquency among children whose parents had divorced. The study found that post-divorce conflict and reduced quality of parenting were associated with these problems.[113]

- A 2001 study based on national data found that divorces in high-conflict marriages have a neutral or beneficial effect on children. Children from low-conflict families who experience parental divorce, however, suffer significant adverse effects in the areas of psychological and social well-being.[114]

- A 2002 study of 238 divorcing mothers and their sons reveals that an increased number of family structure transitions correlates with a decrease in academic scores and an increase in defiant and destructive behavior and tendency toward depression.[115]

- A 2002 study found that, compared to children with married parents, children with divorced parents are more likely to have behavior problems such as aggression or acting-out. Researchers suggested that children's behavior problems are a response to divorced parents' poor parenting, which is a result of the economic and psychological stresses of single parenthood.[116]

SNAPSHOT 2
Children of divorce often experience diminished contact with their fathers.

- A 2003 study of fathers living apart from their children found that nearly half were responsible for more than one set of non-resident children, and that these fathers were less likely to pay child support than were those with only one set of non-resident children. Also, cohabiting or remarried fathers who had biological children with their spouse or partner were less likely to visit their nonresident children than were fathers with no new children.[117]

THE EFFECTS OF DIVORCE ON YOUNG ADULTS

Divorce is a life-transforming experience. After divorce, childhood is different. Adolescence is different. Adult-hood—with the decision to marry or not and have children or not—is different. Whether the final outcome is good or bad, the whole trajectory of an individual's life is profoundly altered by the divorce experience.

—Judith Wallerstein, Julia M.
Lewis and Sandra Blakeslee
*The Unexpected Legacy of Divorce:
A 25 Year Landmark Study*

SNAPSHOT 1
Children of divorced parents often acquire less education.

- A 1994 national study found that children of divorce are more likely to drop out of high school than are children of continuously married parents.[118]

- Compared to children raised by widowed mothers, children from divorced single-mother homes are significantly less likely either to complete high school or to attend or to graduate from college, according to a 2000 study.[119]

SNAPSHOT 2
Among young adults, parental divorce often leads to premarital sex, unwed pregnancy and cohabitation.

- A 2004 study found that young women who experience parental divorce are twice as likely to cohabit before marriage and to have a child out of wedlock than are children raised by their married biological parents.[120]

- Compared to children in intact families, young people who experience parental divorce in childhood are more likely to have sexual intercourse at an earlier age and almost twice as likely to become parents before marriage, according to a British study.[121]

- According to a 2003 study, young women raised by single, step- or cohabiting parents are much more likely to cohabit during their first union than are those raised by their married biological parents. In addition, the more transitions in family living arrangements a woman experiences as a child, the higher her risk of cohabiting.[122]

SNAPSHOT 3

Young adults from divorced homes often have negative attitudes toward marriage and mistrust in dating relationships.

- In a 1999 study, college students with divorced parents were more likely than children from intact families to say they would divorce if there was "a lot of arguing," "no love," or "no magic" in their marriage.[123]

- A 1997 study revealed that college students from divorced families did not trust their romantic partners as much or love them as selflessly as did students from intact families.[124]

- A study of 18-year-olds and their mothers found that children of divorced parents were more likely to endorse premarital sex and cohabitation, to have negative attitudes toward marriage, and to prefer a smaller family size than were children with continuously married or widowed parents.[125]

SNAPSHOT 4

Young adult women from divorced homes are at increased risk for developing psychological problems.

- A study of 18- to 23-year-olds found that female children of recently divorced parents experienced more symptoms and greater frequency of depression, and were 50 percent more likely to say they needed psychological help, than were those with continuously married parents. They were also twice as likely to report that others thought they needed psychological help.[126]

SNAPSHOT 5

Young adults with divorced parents often experience diminished contact with their fathers.

- A 1994 study of young adults age 18-23 found that those with recently divorced parents had less contact with their fathers than did those in intact families. Among young adults not living with their parents, one out of seven children with divorced parents had less than monthly contact with his or her father.[127]

- Young adult daughters of divorced parents report less intimacy with their fathers than do their peers from intact families.[128]

THE EFFECTS OF DIVORCE ON ADULT CHILDREN OF DIVORCE

Contrary to what we have long thought, the major impact of divorce does not occur during childhood or adolescence. Rather, it rises in adulthood as serious romantic relationships move center stage. When it comes time to choose a life mate and build a new family, the effects of divorce crescendo.

—Judith Wallerstein, Julia M. Lewis
and Sandra Blakeslee
*The Unexpected Legacy of Divorce: A 25
Year Landmark Study*

SNAPSHOT 1
Adult children of divorce are likely to suffer emotionally.

- A 33-year study revealed that children who experienced a parental divorce in their childhood or adolescence were likely to experience emotional problems such as depression or anxiety well into their twenties or early thirties.[129]

- A 17-year longitudinal study of two generations found that, compared to children raised in intact homes, children with divorced parents were likely to experience lower self-esteem, less happiness and more psychological distress as adults.[130]

- A 2003 study of 1,104 adults found that those who experienced parental divorce by age seven were twice as likely to suffer from major depression as adults (regardless of whether their mother remarried) than those who were raised in intact families.[131]

- A 2001 study of 17,337 adults in San Diego, California found that, compared to those raised in intact families, adults who had experienced parental separation or divorce in childhood were twice as likely to attempt suicide.[132]

SNAPSHOT 2
Adult children of divorce are more likely both to experience greater conflict in their own marriages and to divorce.

- A national longitudinal study found that married couples are at higher risk for divorce when one spouse is a child of divorce. When both spouses' parents are divorced, their risk for divorce is further increased.[133]

- Children of divorce are twice as likely to divorce as are the offspring of continuously married parents, according to a national longitudinal study of two generations. The authors suggest that their higher risk of divorce is due to a weaker commitment to lifelong marriage.[134]

- A study of three generations found that daughters of divorced parents are at much higher risk for divorce than are girls with married parents.[135]

SNAPSHOT 3
Adult children of divorce are likely to achieve less both educationally and economically.

- Compared to children raised by widowed mothers, adults who grew up in divorced single-mother homes are more likely to take lower status jobs and less likely to report happiness in adulthood.[136]

- Men and women who were raised by their married biological parents have more years of education and higher earnings than do children raised in other family structures. Women suffer educationally when they experience parental divorce in childhood, leading to disadvantages in occupational status and earnings.[137]

SNAPSHOT 4
Adult children of divorce are likely to experience weak family relationships.

- Adults who have experienced parental divorce are less likely to have frequent contact and close relationships with their parents than are adult children from intact families.[138]

- A 1999 study of single elderly persons found that, compared to the divorced, widowed persons gave twice as much financial assistance to their children, and they were more likely to live with their children.[139]

THE EFFECTS OF DIVORCE ON SPOUSES WHO DIVORCE

SNAPSHOT 1
Divorced men and women have poorer physical and mental health.

- Compared to married women, divorced women experience more frequent and serious depression.[140]

- A 2001 national study of nearly 800 families found that, compared to married mothers with biological children, divorced single mothers report more depression, lower self-esteem, lower self-efficacy and less satisfaction with their lives.[141]

- Divorced fathers are more likely to be depressed than are continuously married fathers. Divorced fathers who do not live with their children are likely to experience a decline in the quality of their relationships with their children, while those who live with their children are likely to be less happy than are married or nonresident fathers.[142]

- Data from the National Survey of Family and Households indicates that married people report less depression and fewer alcohol problems than do never-married, separated, divorced or widowed persons. Individuals who marry for the first time or remarry experience a significant decrease in depression, while those who separate or divorce become more depressed.[143]

- A 2000 study comparing the health of married, widowed, divorced, cohabiting and never-married adults, ages 51-61, found that divorcees had the worst overall health. Compared to married persons, the divorced had a higher prevalence of health problems in 17 out of a possible 18 categories, which included hypertension, diabetes, stroke, cancer, heart disease, arthritis and psychiatric problems.[144]

- A 2000 national study found that divorced and separated men and women are more than twice as likely as married persons to commit suicide. Divorced men are nearly two-and-a-half times more likely to die from suicide than are married men.[145]

SNAPSHOT 2
Divorce renders women financially vulnerable.

- Compared to widowed mothers, divorced mothers hold lower status jobs, experience more financial stress and are less likely to be full-time homemakers.[146]

- The income of a mother and child decreases by about 50 percent after separation.[147]

- When divorce or separation occurs, women, on average, experience a 50 percent decline in their family income, and at least a 20 percent decline in their per capita income. Men, on the other hand, experience only modest declines in family income while their per capita income increases 50 to 90 percent.[148]

SNAPSHOT 3
Remarriage is common among divorced people, but it often leads again to divorce.

- Fify-four percent of divorced women remarry within 5 years and 75 percent remarry within 10 years.[149]

- Fifteen percent of second marriages dissolve after three years and 23 percent after five years.[150]

WHAT THE POLLS SAY ABOUT DIVORCE

SNAPSHOT 1
Americans view divorce as a major problem.

- Most Americans (78%) see the high rate of divorce and the breakup of families as a serious problem, according to a 1999 poll.

Question: "I'm going to read a list of things that some people consider to be problems facing American families today. For each one, please tell me how serious a problem you feel it is for families today—very serious, fairly serious, just somewhat serious, or not much of a problem at all. . . . The high rate of divorce and the breakup of families."

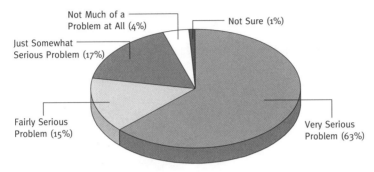

Not Much of a Problem at All (4%)

Not Sure (1%)

Just Somewhat Serious Problem (17%)

Fairly Serious Problem (15%)

Very Serious Problem (63%)

Source: NBC News, *Wall Street Journal* [151]

- In 1997, almost half of those surveyed said the main reason for increased divorce is that marriage is not taken seriously by couples.

Question: "What is the main reason for the increase in the number of divorces?"

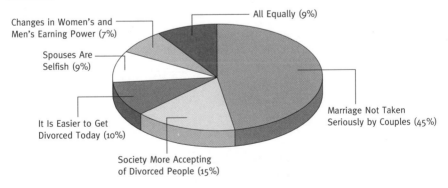

All Equally (9%)

Changes in Women's and Men's Earning Power (7%)

Spouses Are Selfish (9%)

It Is Easier to Get Divorced Today (10%)

Society More Accepting of Divorced People (15%)

Marriage Not Taken Seriously by Couples (45%)

Source: Time, CNN [152]

SNAPSHOT 2
Most Americans think that divorce harms children.

- In a 2000 poll, 64 percent said that children are "almost always" or are "frequently" harmed when parents get divorced.

Question: "When parents get divorced, are children harmed?"

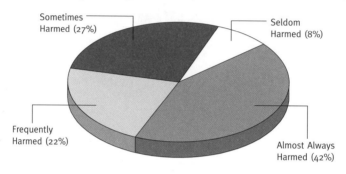

Sometimes Harmed (27%)

Seldom Harmed (8%)

Frequently Harmed (22%)

Almost Always Harmed (42%)

Source: Time, CNN [153]

- In 2000, 33 percent agreed that parents should stay together for the sake of the children even if the marriage isn't working, compared to only 21 percent who said the same in 1981.

Question: "Do you agree or disagree that for the children's sake, parents should stay together and not get a divorce, even if the marriage isn't working?"

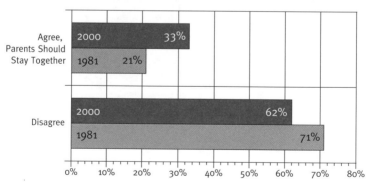

Agree, Parents Should Stay Together — 2000: 33%; 1981: 21%

Disagree — 2000: 62%; 1981: 71%

0% 10% 20% 30% 40% 50% 60% 70% 80%

Source: Time, CNN [154]

SNAPSHOT 3

Most Americans think that it should be more difficult for those with children to obtain a divorce.

- A 2002 poll shows that 49 percent think a divorce should be harder to obtain than it is now.

Question: "Should divorce in this country be easier or harder to obtain than it is now?"

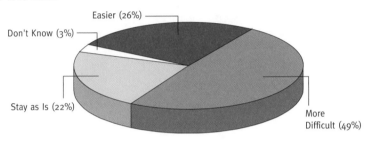

Easier (26%)

Don't Know (3%)

Stay as Is (22%)

More Difficult (49%)

Source: General Social Survey [155]

- A 1997 poll found that 61 percent believe it should be harder than it is now for married couples with young children to get a divorce.

Question: "Should it be harder than it is now for married couples with young children to get a divorce?"

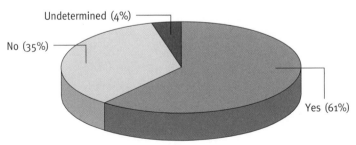

Undetermined (4%)

No (35%)

Yes (61%)

Source: Time, CNN [156]

- In a 2000 poll, 78 percent supported a proposal to require married couples with children who are considering a divorce to obtain counseling before a divorce would be granted.

Question: "Please tell me if you approve or disapprove of each proposal. Requiring counseling to married couples with children who are considering a divorce before the divorce is granted."

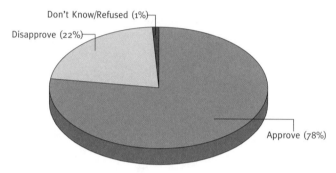

Don't Know/Refused (1%)

Disapprove (22%)

Approve (78%)

Source: Wirthlin Worldwide [157]

CHAPTER 9

Single-Parent Families

Tonight, about 40 percent of American children will go to sleep in homes in which their fathers do not live. Before they reach the age of eighteen, more than half of our nation's children are likely to spend at least a significant portion of their childhoods living apart from their fathers.

—David Blankenhorn
*Fatherless America: Confronting
Our Most Urgent Social Problem*

BY THE NUMBERS: SINGLE-PARENT FAMILIES

SNAPSHOT 1

The number of children living in single-parent families has more than doubled since 1970.

- In 1970, 8.2 million children lived in a single-parent family, compared to 19.8 million in 2002.

Number of Children in Single-Parent Families, 1960-2002

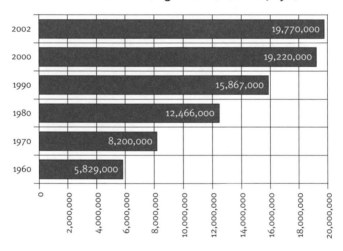

YEAR	NUMBER OF CHILDREN LIVING WITH ONE PARENT
1960	5,829,000
1970	8,200,000
1975	11,245,000
1980	12,466,000
1985	14,635,000
1990	15,867,000
1993	17,872,000
1995	18,938,000
1997	19,799,000
2000	19,220,000
2002	19,770,000

Source:
U.S. Census Bureau[158]

SNAPSHOT 2
One out of four children lives with a single parent.

- Between 1970 and 2002, the percentage of children living with a single parent increased from 11.9 percent to 27.3 percent.

Children Living with a Single Parent, Historical

Year	Number of Children Under 18	Percent Living with a Single Parent*
1940	40,435,000	10.3%
1950	46,506,000	8.9%
1960	64,586,000	10.3%
1970	69,162,000	11.9%
1980	63,427,000	19.7%
1990	64,137,000	24.7%
1996	71,494,000	25.4%
2000	72,012,000	26.7%
2002	72,321,000	27.3%

*Includes single parents who are cohabiting and single stepparents.

Source: U.S. Census Bureau [159]

SNAPSHOT 3
Most children in single-parent families live with their mother.

- In 2002, 83 percent of children in single-parent families lived with their mother.[160]

- From 1960 to 2002, the number of children living with only their mother increased more than three-fold, from 5.1 million to 16.5 million.

- Among children living in single-mother families, 4 percent lived with their never-married mother in 1960, compared to 42 percent in 2002.

Percent of Children Living with Mother Only, by Mother's Marital Status, 1960 and 2002

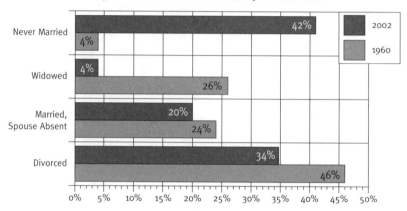

Percent of Children Living with Mother Only, by Mother's Marital Status, 1960-2002

YEAR	TOTAL NUMBER OF CHILDREN LIVING WITH MOTHER ONLY	PERCENT LIVING WITH DIVORCED MOTHER	PERCENT LIVING WITH MARRIED MOTHER, SPOUSE ABSENT	PERCENT LIVING WITH NEVER-MARRIED MOTHER	PERCENT LIVING WITH WIDOWED MOTHER
1960	5,105,000	46%	24%	4%	26%
1970	7,452,000	31%	43%	7%	19%
1980	11,406,000	42%	32%	15%	11%
1990	13,874,000	37%	25%	31%	7%
1993	15,586,000	36%	24%	35%	4%
1995	16,477,000	37%	24%	36%	4%
1997	16,740,000	35%	22%	39%	3%
2000	16,162,000	35%	20%	41%	4%
2002	16,472,000	34%	20%	42%	4%

Source: U.S. Census Bureau [161]

SNAPSHOT 4

In recent years, the percentage of children living with a single mother has declined.

- According to a 2001 study, the percentage of children under 18 living with a single mother dropped eight percent from 1995 - 2000. Between 1985 and 1990, the percentage of children living with a single mother remained constant.[162]

Percent of Children Under Age 18 Living with a Single Mother, 1985-2000

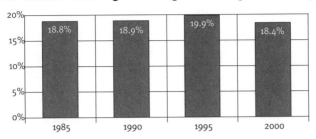

Source: Center on Budget and Policy Priorities [163]

SNAPSHOT 5
The number of children living in single-father families has more than quadrupled since 1960.

- The number of children living with only their father in 2002 (3.3 million) was more than four times greater than the number in 1960 (724,000).

- Among children living with their father only in 2002, similar numbers lived with their divorced father (41%) or with their never-married father (38 percent).

Percent of Children Living with Father Only, by Father's Marital Status, 1960 and 2002

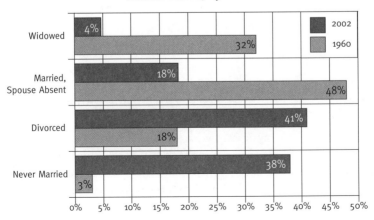

Percent of Children Living with Father Only, by Father's Marital Status, 1960-2002

YEAR	TOTAL NUMBER OF CHILDREN LIVING WITH FATHER ONLY	PERCENT LIVING WITH DIVORCED FATHER	PERCENT LIVING WITH MARRIED FATHER, SPOUSE ABSENT	PERCENT LIVING WITH WIDOWED FATHER	PERCENT LIVING WITH NEVER-MARRIED FATHER
1960	724,000	18%	48%	32%	3%
1970	748,000	24%	38%	34%	4%
1980	1,060,000	49%	27%	17%	7%
1990	1,993,000	50%	18%	8%	24%
1993	2,286,000	42%	21%	5%	33%
1995	2,461,000	48%	18%	5%	28%
1997	3,059,000	45%	19%	4%	31%
2000	3,058,000	43%	19%	5%	33%
2002	3,297,000	41%	18%	4%	38%

Source: U.S. Census Bureau [164]

THE EFFECTS OF SINGLE PARENTING

Adolescents who have lived apart from one of their parents during some period of childhood are twice as likely to drop out of high school, twice as likely to have a child before age twenty, and one-and-a-half times as likely to be "idle"—out of school and out of work—in their late teens and early twenties.

—Sara McLanahan and Gary Sandefur
Growing Up with a Single Parent: What Hurts, What Helps

FAMILY RESEARCH COUNCIL

THE EFFECTS OF SINGLE PARENTING ON CHILDREN

SNAPSHOT 1

Children in single-parent families are likely to suffer economically.

- Children living with a single mother are six times more likely to live in poverty than are children with married parents.[165]

- In 2002, only 7 percent of married-couple families with children under 18 were below the poverty level, compared to 34 percent of families headed by a single mother.[166]

- In 2001, 26 percent of white single mothers with children under 18 were below the poverty level, as well as 41 percent of black single mothers and 43 percent of Hispanic single mothers.[167]

- A 2002 study based on national data of over 10,000 adults with children under 18 found that the poverty rate among single parents is three times higher than that of married parents. Also, single parents are much more likely to experience material hardships such as lack of food, poor housing and utility shutoffs.[168]

SNAPSHOT 2

Children in single-parent families are likely to struggle academically.

- A 2003 study of 11 industrialized countries found that children living in single-parent families earn lower math and science scores than do children in two-parent families. The association between single parenthood and low test scores was strongest among children in the United States and New Zealand.[169]

- A 1998 study based on national data found that children who live in single-parent families demonstrate less aptitude for mathematics and reading than do children raised in two-parent families.[170]

SNAPSHOT 3
Children in single-parent families are more likely to develop emotional and behavioral problems.

- According to a Swedish study of almost a million children, children raised by single parents are more than twice as likely as those raised in two-parent homes to suffer from a serious psychiatric disorder, to commit or attempt suicide or to develop an alcohol addiction. Girls from single-parent homes are three times more likely to become addicted to drugs and boys are four times more likely.[171]

- A 1998 study of youth age 12-17 found that those in single-parent families and stepfamilies are more likely to be sexually experienced at an earlier age than are children who live with both biological parents.[172]

- A 1998 study of families with a 6- to 10-year-old child revealed that children from single-parent families are more likely to be fearful and depressed; to lie, cheat and destroy property; and to associate with troublemakers than are children of married parents.[173]

- A 2000 study based on data collected from more than 30,000 children's visits to pediatricians and family practitioners in 1979 and 1996 found that children from single-parent households were twice as likely to have emotional and behavioral problems as were children living with both parents. This study concluded that the significant increase of such psychosocial problems in children age 4-15 between 1979 and

1996 proportionally reflected the increase in the number of single-parent families during these years.[174]

SNAPSHOT 4
Children living in single-parent families are more likely to experience abuse.

- A 1998 study found that children in single-parent families are more than twice as likely to be physically abused as are children living with both biological parents.[175]

- A 1996 national study on child abuse found that children in single-parent families had a 77 percent greater risk of harm by physical abuse and an 87 percent greater risk of harm due to physical neglect than did children living in two-parent homes.[176]

THE EFFECTS OF SINGLE PARENTING ON PARENTS

SNAPSHOT 1
Single mothers are more likely to live in poverty and to have psychological problems than are married mothers.

- According to a 1999 study, never-married mothers with at least two children are almost six times more likely than are married mothers to be on welfare. They are also 40 percent less likely to be working full time, and, if working, more likely to have a low income.[177]

- A 1998 study of the economic status of mothers at the time they gave birth found that, among those who were unwed and age 20 or older, 60 percent depended on welfare after the birth of their child.[178]

- In 2001, the median income of a single mother with at least one child under 18 was $21,997, compared to $65,203 for a married couple with one or more children under 18.[179]

- A 2003 study of 2,921 mothers found that single mothers were more than twice as likely as married mothers to report an episode of depression during the prior year. Single mothers also reported higher levels of stress, less perceived social support, fewer contacts with family and friends, and less involvement in church or social groups.[180]

- A 1997 Canadian study found that single mothers who have never married or are separated or divorced are nearly three times more likely than are married mothers to have experienced major depression.[181]

SNAPSHOT 2
Single fathers are likely to fare poorly economically and to have infrequent contact with their children.

- A 1998 study of more than 4,000 men found that those who fathered children out of wedlock attained less education, earned less and worked fewer weeks per year than did those who had not fathered children outside marriage.[182]

- In 2001, the median income of a single father with at least one child under 18 was $31,932, compared to $65,203 for married couples with children under 18.[183]

- A 2003 study of fathers living apart from their children found that nearly half were responsible for more than one set of non-resident children, and that these fathers were less likely to pay child support than were those with only one set of non-resident children. Also, cohabiting or remarried fathers who had biological children with their spouse or partner were less likely to visit their non-resident children than were fathers with no new children.[184]

WHAT THE POLLS SAY ABOUT SINGLE-PARENT FAMILIES

SNAPSHOT 1
Americans think single parenting is hard on both children and parents.

- Most Americans think children in single-parent families are disadvantaged compared to children in two-parent families, according to a 1997 poll.

Question: "Do you think that children who grow up in one-parent families are just as well-off, somewhat worse off, or much worse off than children who grow up in two-parent families?"

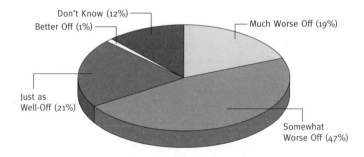

Don't Know (12%)
Better Off (1%)
Much Worse Off (19%)
Just as Well-Off (21%)
Somewhat Worse Off (47%)

Source: Roper Center [185]

- An overwhelming majority of Americans believe that single parenting is the most difficult task a parent can undertake.

Question: "How much do you agree or disagree with the following? To be a single parent has got to be the most stressful thing in the world."

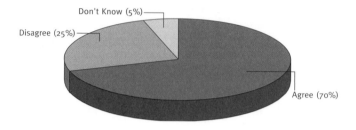

Don't Know (5%)

Disagree (25%)

Agree (70%)

Source: Public Agenda [186]

SNAPSHOT 2
Most Americans see the rise of single-parent households as a problem.

- A 1999 poll found that 64 percent of Americans think the rise of single-parent households is a serious problem.

Question: "How serious a problem do you feel ... the rise of single-parent households ... is for families today—very serious, fairly serious, just somewhat serious, or not much of a problem at all?"

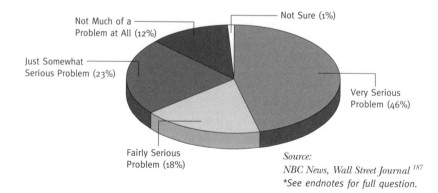

Not Much of a Problem at All (12%)

Not Sure (1%)

Just Somewhat Serious Problem (23%)

Very Serious Problem (46%)

Fairly Serious Problem (18%)

Source:
NBC News, Wall Street Journal [187]
*See endnotes for full question.

- A 1999 poll found that 77 percent of Americans believe that increases in divorce and single parenting have weakened family ties.

Question: "In general, do you think that because of such things as divorce, more working mothers, single parents etc., family ties in the U.S. are breaking down, or don't you think so?"

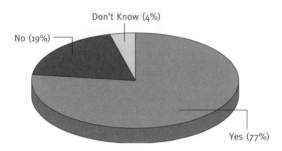

Source: *New York Times* [188]

- Most Americans think welfare programs that encourage single-parent families and teenage pregnancy are a serious problem, according to a 1999 poll.

Question: "I'm going to describe different problems and ask if you think each is a serious problem facing today's kids. Is that problem very serious, somewhat serious, not too serious, or not serious at all for today's kids? ... Welfare programs that encourage single-parent families and teenage pregnancy."

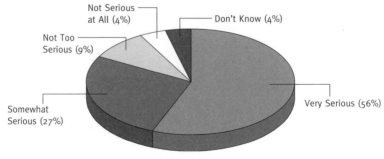

Source: *Public Agenda* [189]

- Over half of all Americans think that high numbers of single-parent families are a major cause of poverty.

Question: "Please tell me if this is a major cause of poverty, a minor cause of poverty, or not a cause at all ... too many single-parent families ..."

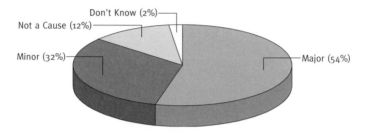

Source: International Communications Research [190]

CHAPTER 10

Stepfamilies

*In families where the mother remarries or cohabits with an
adult male, the quality of parenting is still likely to be lower
than in families with two biological parents.*

—Sara McLanahan and Gary Sandefur
*Growing Up with a Single Parent: What
Hurts, What Helps*

BY THE NUMBERS: STEPFAMILIES

SNAPSHOT 1
In 2000, 4.4 million children under 18 lived in a stepfamily.

- According to the 2000 Census, 5.2 percent of children of all ages live in a stepfamily.

Stepchildren, 2000

Total number of all children of householders	83,714,107
Total number of stepchildren (all ages)	4,384,581
Stepchildren under age 18	3,292,301
Stepchildren under age 6	328,378
Stepchildren age 6-11	1,271,122
Stepchildren age 12-14	847,130
Stepchildren age 15-17	845,671
Stepchildren age 18 and over	1,092,280
Stepchildren age 18 to 24	778,441
Stepchildren age 25 and over	313,839

Source: U.S. Census Bureau [191]

THE EFFECTS OF STEPPARENTING ON PARENTS AND CHILDREN

SNAPSHOT 1
Stepfamilies are less cohesive and less stable than intact families.

- Sixty percent of stepfamilies are disrupted by divorce and 25 percent dissolve within the first two years, according to a longitudinal study of over 200 stepfamilies.[192]

- A 1995 study based on national data found that 54 percent of children in stepfamilies experience a parental separation within 10 years.[193]

- A 2001 study found that married fathers with biological children spend significantly more time with their children and are more likely to report close family ties than do stepfathers and remarried fathers with biological children.[194]

SNAPSHOT 2
Children in stepfamilies are at increased risk for experiencing physical or sexual abuse.

- Compared to girls raised in intact families, girls living in stepfamilies are twice as likely to be sexually abused not only by their stepfather but also by "other men prior to the arrival of the stepfather in the home."[195]

- According to a 1997 review of child abuse studies, children in stepfamilies, especially girls, are at higher risk for sexual abuse than are those living with their biological parents. Both boys and girls living in stepfamilies are likely to be physically abused.[196]

- Children living with a stepfather are more than three times as likely to be sexually abused as are children in other households.[197]

SNAPSHOT 3
Academic performance and support often are deficient among children in stepfamilies.

- A 1999 study found that children of divorce living in step-families earn lower scores on academic achievement tests than do children raised in intact families or in divorced single-parent homes. Researchers believe that "remarriage following divorce … may actually have a negative effect on academic achievement." [198]

- When compared to children in nuclear families, children raised in mother-stepfather families are 80 percent more likely to repeat a grade and twice as likely to be suspended or expelled from school.[199]

- Children raised in stepfamilies are less likely to attend college than are children living with married parents. They are more likely to leave home early, to live independently, to join the military or to work, to cohabit or to raise a child on their own.[200]

SNAPSHOT 4
Children in stepfamilies are more prone to abuse alcohol and drugs than are children in intact families.

- A 1998 study found that adolescents in stepfamilies are much more likely to report marijuana use than are adolescents living with both biological parents (1.5 times more likely for children in mother-stepfather households and more than twice as likely in father-step-mother households). Drunkenness and illicit drug use among youth are most likely in father-stepmother families and in single-father families.[201]

- According to a 1998 study, adolescents from stepfamilies reported significantly more frequent drug use in 8th and 10th grades than did adolescents in intact families.[202]

SNAPSHOT 5
Stepchildren frequently struggle emotionally and behaviorally.

- A study of 5,201 adolescents found that, compared to those living in intact families, adolescents living in single-parent or stepfamilies were more likely to report feeling lonely. Adolescents who felt less connected to their parents, engaged in fewer activities with their parents and experienced less parental presence at key times during the day were more likely to feel lonely.[203]

- Children in stepfamilies are much more likely than are children in intact families to experience emotional and behavioral problems, to need psychological help and to report poor health.[204]

- Compared to teens raised by their married biological parents, teens living in stepfamilies are more likely to be expelled from school, to engage in delinquency and to earn lower grade point averages. They also have problems getting along with students and teachers and completing homework assignments.[205]

SNAPSHOT 6
The overall parent-child relationship is weakened in stepfamilies.

- Children living with their married biological parents spend more time with their father and receive more affection and warmth from him than do those living with a step- or a single father or with a cohabiting father figure.[206]

- A 1999 study of single elderly persons found that, compared to those with only biological children, those with stepchildren were less likely to live with their children or to give financial assistance to them. Also, 68 percent of the elderly persons with only biological children received help from their children with basic activities (such as bathing, meal preparation, shopping and managing finances), compared to only 30 percent of those with only stepchildren.[207]

- Remarried parents are less likely to exchange social support (such as advice, emotional support, and help with transportation or housework) with their adult children than are parents in a first marriage.[208]

SNAPSHOT 7
Stepparents encounter many difficulties in their new role.

- Parents of stepchildren and those with non-custodial children under 18 are likely to report less satisfaction in parenting than are parents in their first marriage living with biological children.[209]

- A 1996 study found that stepmothers especially experience greater difficulty in parenting their stepchildren than in parenting their biological children.[210]

WHAT THE POLLS SAY ABOUT STEPFAMILIES

SNAPSHOT 1
Americans view stepparenting as a challenging role.

Question: "I'm going to ask how good a job you think some different types of parents can do raising kids today. What about stepmothers . . . do you think most can do a good job as parents today, some can, very few can, or none of them can do a good job as parents today?"

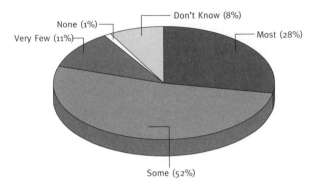

Source: Princeton Survey [211]

CHAPTER 5 Adult Unwed Sex & Adultery

1   Edward O. Laumann, et al., *The Social Organization of Sexuality: Sexual Practices in the United States* (Chicago: University of Chicago Press, 1994), p. 214.

2   Ibid., p. 329.

3   Other researchers contend that as many as 40 to 60 percent of men and women have committed adultery. The data included in this chapter come from *The Social Organization of Sexuality*, published by the University of Chicago, which is regarded as the most authoritative and carefully designed recent survey on sex.

4   Ibid., p. 216.

5   Ibid., p. 364.

6   Ibid., p. 368.

7   Tim B. Heaton, "Factors Contributing to Increasing Marital Stability in the United States," *Journal of Family Issues* 23 (April 2002): 392-409.

8   Paul R. Amato and Denise Previti, "People's Reasons for Divorcing: Gender, Social Class, the Life Course and Adjustment," *Journal of Family Issues* 24 (July 2003): 602-626.

9   Lawrence B. Finer, Jacqueline E. Darroch and Susheela Singh, "Sexual Partnership Patterns as a Behavioral Risk Factor For Sexually Transmitted Diseases," *Family Planning Perspectives* 31 (1999): 228-236.

10 The Kaiser Family Foundation, *Sexually Transmitted Diseases in the United States*, February 2000, p. 1.

11 Ibid.

12 The Kaiser Family Foundation, *Sexually Transmitted Diseases in the United States*, June 2003, p.1.

13 Centers for Disease Control and Prevention, *Tracking the Hidden Epidemics: Trends in STDs in the United States: 2000.*

14 Ibid.

15 Ibid., p. 2, and The Kaiser Family Foundation, *HPV (Human Papillomavirus) and Cervical Cancer*, July 2001, p. 1.

16 The Kaiser Family Foundation, *HPV (Human Papillomavirus) and Cervical Cancer.*

17 Harrell W. Chesson, et al., "The Estimated Direct Medical Cost of Sexually Transmitted Diseases Among American Youth, 2000," *Perspectives on Sexual and Reproductive Health* 36 (January/February 2004): 11-19.

18 The Alan Guttmacher Institute, "Induced Abortion," *Facts in Brief*, 2003 and Kaiser Family Foundation, *Fact Sheet: Abortion in the U.S.*, January 2003.

19 Gallup Poll, May 5-7, 2003.

20   General Social Survey, National Opinion Research Center, February 6 – June 26, 2002.

21   Gallup Poll, May 5-7, 2003.

CHAPTER 6 Adult Unwed Childbearing

22   Joyce A. Martin, et al., *Births: Final Data for 2002*, National Vital Statistics Reports 52, December 17, 2003, p.10.

23   Stephanie Ventura, et al., *Nonmarital Childbearing in the United States, 1940-99*, National Vital Statistics Reports 48, October 18, 2000, National Center for Health Statistics, Table 1 and Joyce A. Martin, et al., *Births Final Data for 2002*, p. 10.

24   Amara Bachu, *Trends in Premarital Childbearing 1930 to 1994*, Current Population Reports, P23-197, October 1999, U.S. Census Bureau, p. 3.

25   Ibid., Table 1.

26   Ibid.

27   Ibid.

28   Barbara Downs, *Fertility of American Women: June 2002*, Current Population Reports, P20-548, U.S. Census Bureau, October 2003, Table 3.

29   National Center for Health Statistics, *Report to Congress on Out-of-Wedlock Childbearing*, (PHS) 95-1257, September 1995, Tables I-2 and III-7 and Joyce A. Martin, et al., *Births: Final Data for 2002*, Tables C and 18.

30   Stephanie J. Ventura, et al., *Nonmarital Childbearing in the United States, 1940-99*, Table 4, Joyce A. Martin, et al., *Births: Final Data for 2000*, Table 17 and Joyce A. Martin, et al., *Births: Final Data for 2002*, Table 18.

31   Stephanie Ventura, et al., *Nonmarital Childbearing in the United States, 1940-99*, Table 3 and Joyce A. Martin, et al., *Births: Final Data for 2002*, Table 18.

32   Joyce A. Martin, et al., *Births: Final Data for 2002*, Table 19.

33   Larry Bumpass and Hsien-Hen Lu, "Trends in Cohabitation and Implications for Children's Family Contexts in the U.S.," NSFH Working Paper No. 83, Center for Demography and Ecology University of Wisconsin-Madison, June 1999, pp. 16-17.

34   Susan G. Timmer and Terri L. Orbuch, "The Links Between Premarital Parenthood, Meanings of Marriage and Marital Outcomes," *Family Relations* 50 (April 2001): 178-185.

35   Anne K. Driscoll, et al., "Nonmarital Childbearing Among Adult Women," *Journal of Marriage and the Family* 61 (February 1999): 178-187.

36   Sara McLanahan and Irwin Garfinkel, "The Fragile Families and Child Wellbeing Study Baseline Report," August 2001, p. 3, Available at *http:// crcw.princeton.edu /fragilefamilies/nationalreport.pdf.*

37   Daniel Lichter, Deborah Roempke Graefe, et al., "Is Marriage a Panacea? Union Formation Among Economically Disadvantaged Unwed Mothers," *Social Problems* 50 (2003): 60-86.

38   Deborah Roempke Graefe and Daniel T. Lichter, "Marriage Among Unwed Mothers: Whites, Blacks and Hispanics Compared," *Perspectives on Sexual and Reproductive Health* 34 (November/December 2002): 286-293.

39 Daniel Lichter, Deborah Roempke Graefe, et al., "Is Marriage a Panacea? Union Formation Among Economically Disadvantaged Unwed Mothers."

40 Steven Nock, "The Consequences of Premarital Fatherhood," *American Sociological Review* 63 (1998): 250-263, as cited in *Family Planning Perspectives* 30 (September/October 1998): 248-249.

41 Kei M. Nomaguchi and Melissa A. Milkie, "Costs and Rewards of Children: The Effects of Becoming a Parent on Adults' Lives," *Journal of Marriage and Family* 65 (May 2003): 356-374.

42 Tom W. Smith, "The Emerging Family in the 21st Century," General Social Survey No. 42, National Opinion Research Center, November 24, 1999.

43 Gallup Poll, May 5-7, 2003.

44 Heather Mason, "Are Out-of-Wedlock Births Morally Acceptable?" The Gallup Organization, July 15, 2003.

45 Ibid.

CHAPTER 7 Cohabitation

46 U.S. Census Bureau, "Unmarried-Couple Households, by Presence of Children: 1960 to Present," Table UC-1, June 12, 2003.

47 David Popenoe and Barbara Dafoe Whitehead, *Should We Live Together? What Young Adults Need to Know about Cohabitation before Marriage*, The National Marriage Project, January, 1999, p. 3.

48 Pamela Smock, "Cohabitation in the United States: An Appraisal of Research Themes, Findings, and Implications," *Annual Review of Sociology* 26 (2000).

49 U.S. Census Bureau, *Statistical Abstract of the United States*, various years. Percent calculations by the author.

50 U.S. Census Bureau, "Unmarried-Couple Households, by Presence of Children: 1960 to Present." Percent calculations by the author.

51 Tavis Simmons and Martin O'Connell, "Married-Couple and Unmarried-Partner Households: 2000," *Census 2000 Special Reports*, U.S Census Bureau, CENSR-5, February 2003, Table 4.

52 David Popenoe and Barbara Dafoe Whitehead, *Should We Live Together?* p. 7.

53 Amara Bachu, *Trends in Premarital Childbearing: 1930 to 1994*, p. 7.

54 Ibid.

55 Lynne M. Casper and Suzanne M. Bianchi, *Continuity and Change in the American Family* (California: Sage Publications, 2002), p. 59.

56 These figures include cohabiting relationships that became marriages. National Center for Health Statistics, *Cohabitation, Marriage, Divorce, and Remarriage in the United States*, Series 23, No. 22, July 2002, p. 14 and Table 15.

57 Ibid, Table 21.

58 Georgina Binstock and Arland Thornton, "Separations, Reconciliations and Living Apart in Cohabiting and Marital Unions," *Journal of Marriage and Family* 65 (May 2003): 432-443.

59   Susan L. Brown, "The Effect of Union Type on Psychological Well-Being:
      Depression Among Cohabitors Versus Marrieds," *Journal of Health and Social
      Behavior* 41 (September 2000): 241-255.

60   Steven L. Nock, "A Comparison of Marriages and Cohabiting Relationships,"
      Journal of Family Issues 16 (January 1995): 53-76.

61   Steven Sack and Ross J. Eshleman, "Marital Status and Happiness: A 17-Nation
      Study," *Journal of Marriage and the Family* 60 (May 1998): 527-536.

62   Sonia Miner Salari and Bret M. Baldwin, "Verbal, Physical, and Injurious
      Aggression Among Intimate Couples Over Time," *Journal of Family Issues* 23 (May
      2002): 523-550.

63   Todd K. Shackelford, "Cohabitation, Marriage, and Murder: Women-Killing by
      Male Romantic Partners," *Aggressive Behavior* 27 (2001): 284-291.

64   Alfred DeMaris, et al., "Distal and Proximal Factors in Domestic Violence: A Test of
      an Integrated Model," *Journal of Marriage and Family* 65 (August 2003): 652-667.

65   Kevin B. Skinner, et al., "Cohabitation, Marriage and Remarriage: A Comparison of
      Relationship Quality Over Time," *Journal of Family Issues* 23 (January 2002): 74-90.

66   Susan L. Brown, "Relationship Quality Dynamics of Cohabiting Unions," *Journal of
      Family Issues* 24 (July 2003): 583-601.

67   Judith Treas and Deirdre Giesen, "Sexual Infidelity Among Married and
      Cohabiting Americans," *Journal of Marriage and the Family* 62 (February 2000): 48-60.

68   Robert I. Lerman, "How Do Marriage, Cohabitation and Single Parenthood Affect
      the Material Hardships of Families With Children?" Urban Institute and American
      University, July 2002.

69   Wendy D. Manning and Daniel T. Lichter, "Parental Cohabitation and Children's
      Economic Well-Being," *Journal of Marriage and the Family* 58 (November 1996): 998-
      1010.

70   Lingxin Hao, "Family Structure, Private Transfers, and the Economic Well-Being of
      Families with Children," *Social Forces* 75 (September 1996): 269-292.

71   The National Marriage Project, *The State of Our Unions 2001: The Social Health of
      Marriage in America,* June 2001, p. 22.

72   Arland Thornton, et al., "Reciprocal Effects of Religiosity, Cohabitation and
      Marriage," *American Journal of Sociology* 98 (November 1992): 628-651.

73   Georgina Binstock and Arland Thornton, "Separations, Reconciliations and Living
      Apart in Cohabiting and Marital Unions."

74   David R. Hall and John Z. Zhao, "Cohabitation and Divorce in Canada: Testing the
      Selectivity Hypothesis," *Journal of Marriage and the Family* 57 (May 1995): 421-427.

75   Catherine L. Coban and Stacey Kleinbaum, "Toward a Greater Understanding of
      the Cohabitation Effect: Premarital Cohabitation and Marital Communication,"
      Journal of Marriage and Family 64 (February 2002): 180-192.

76   Claire M. Kamp Dush, et al., "The Relationship Between Cohabitation and Marital
      Quality and Stability: Change Across Cohorts?" *Journal of Marriage and Family* 65
      (August 2003): 539-549.

77 William Axinn and Jennifer Barber, "Living Arrangements and Family Formation in Early Adulthood," *Journal of Marriage and the Family* 59 (August 1997): 595-611.

78 Judith Treas and Deirdre Giesen, "Sexual Infidelity Among Married and Cohabiting Americans."

79 Larry Bumpass and Hsien-Hen Lu, "Trends in Cohabitation and Implications for Children's Family Contexts in the U.S.," p. 14.

80 David Popenoe and Barbara Dafoe Whitehead, *Should We Live Together? What Young Adults Need to Know about Cohabitation before Marriage*, Second Edition, National Marriage Project, 2002, p. 8.

81 "Absent Dads: How Many Live Apart from Their Children," *ISR Update*, University of Michigan Institute for Social Research, Fall 2002.

82 Susan L. Brown, "Child Well-Being in Cohabiting Families," in Alan Booth and Ann C. Crouter, eds., *Just Living Together: Implications of Cohabitation on Families, Children and Social Policy* (New Jersey: Lawrence Erlbaum Associates, 2002), p. 173-187.

83 Gregory Acs and Sandi Nelson, "The Kids Are Alright? Children's Well-Being and the Rise in Cohabitation," The Urban Institute, July 2002.

84 Susan L. Brown, "Child Well-Being in Cohabiting Families."

85 Elizabeth Thomson, et al., "Family Structure and Child Well-being: Economic Resources vs. Parental Behaviors," *Social Forces* 73 (September 1994): 221-242.

86 Sandi Nelson, et al., "Beyond the Two-Parent Family: How Teenagers Fare in Cohabiting Couple and Blended Families," The Urban Institute, May 2001.

87 Wendy D. Manning and Kathleen A. Lamb, "Adolescent Well-Being in Cohabiting, Married, and Single-Parent Families," *Journal of Marriage and Family* 65 (November 2003): 876-893.

88 Wendy D. Manning and Daniel T. Lichter, "Parental Cohabitation and Children's Economic Well-Being."

89 Susan L. Brown, "Child Well-Being in Cohabiting Families."

90 Robert I. Lerman, "How Do Marriage, Cohabitation and Single Parenthood Affect the Material Hardships of Families With Children?"

91 Zogby America Poll, March 15, 2000.

92 Gallup Organization for CNN, *USA Today*, May 18-20, 2001.

93 General Social Survey, National Opinion Research Center, February 6 – June 26, 2002.

94 University of Michigan Institute for Social Research, *ISR Update*, Vol. 2, No. 1, Fall 2002.

95 Jerald G. Bachman, et al., "Monitoring the Future: Questionnaire Responses from the Nation's High School Seniors," The Monitoring the Future Study, Survey Research Center, Institute for Social Research, The University of Michigan, 2002.

CHAPTER 8 Divorce

96 National Marriage Project, *The State of Our Unions 2003: The Social Health of Marriage in America*, June 2003, p. 25.

97   U.S. Census Bureau, *Statistical Abstract of the United States: 1998*, Table No. 156; *Statistical Abstract of the United States: 1985*, Table No. 120; *Statistical Abstract of the United States: 1970*, Table No. 75; and National Marriage Project, *The State of Our Unions 2003: The Social Health of Marriage in America*, June 2003, p. 24.

98   Ibid.

99   Rose M. Kreider and Jason M. Fields, *Number, Timing, and Duration of Marriages and Divorces: 1996*, Current Population Reports, P70-80, U.S. Census Bureau, February 2002, p. 7.

100 Paul A. Nakonezny and Robert D. Shull, "The Effect of No-Fault Divorce Law on the Divorce Rate Across the 50 States and Its Relation to Income, Education, and Religiosity," *Journal of Marriage and the Family* 57 (May 1995): 477-488.

101 Leora Friedburg, "Did Unilateral Divorce Raise Divorce Rates? Evidence from Panel Data," *American Economic Review* 88 (June 1998): 608-627.

102 U.S. Census Bureau, *Statistical Abstract of the United States: 2002*, Table 111.

103 Judith Wallerstein, Julia M. Lewis and Sandra Blakeslee, *The Unexpected Legacy of Divorce: A 25 Year Landmark Study* (New York: Hyperion, 2000), p. xxvi.

104 U.S. Census Bureau, *Statistical Abstract of the United States: 1998*, Table 160 and *Statistical Abstract of the United States: 1985*, Table 120.

105 Sanford L. Braver and Diane O'Connell, *Divorced Dads: Shattering the Myths* (New York: Tarcher/Putnam, 1998), p. 133.

106 Paul Amato and Alan Booth, *A Generation at Risk: Growing Up in an Era of Family Upheaval* (Cambridge: Harvard University Press, 1997), p. 220.

107 Rose M. Kreider and Jason M. Fields, *Number, Timing, and Duration of Marriages and Divorces: 1996*, p. 9.

108 Ibid., p. 3.

109 Matthew D. Bramlett and William D. Mosher, *First Marriage Dissolution, Divorce and Remarriage: United States*, Advance Data, National Center for Health Statistics, May 31, 2001, p. 1.

110 David G. Schramm, "What Could Divorce Be Costing Your State? The Costly Consequences of Divorce in Utah: The Impact on Couples, Communities, and Government," A Preliminary Report, June 25, 2003, Publication in Process, Department of Family, Consumer, and Human Development, Utah State University.

111 Ibid.

112 Judith Wallerstein and Joan B. Kelly, *Surviving the Breakup: How Children and Parents Cope with Divorce* (New York: BasicBooks, 1996), pp. 46-50, 211.

113 Ronald L. Simons, et al., "Explaining the Higher Incidence of Adjustment Problems Among Children of Divorce Compared with Those in Two-Parent Families," *Journal of Marriage and the Family* 61 (November 1999): 1020-1033.

114 Alan Booth and Paul R. Amato, "Parental Predivorce Relations and Offspring Postdivorce Well-Being," *Journal of Marriage and Family* 63 (February 2001): 197-212.

115 Charles R. Martinez Jr. and Marion S. Forgatch, "Adjusting to Change: Linking Family Structure Transitions With Parenting and Boys' Adjustment," *Journal of Family Psychology* 16 (2002): 107-117.

116 Jeanne M. Hilton and Stephan Desrochers, "Children's Behavior Problems in Single-Parent and Married-Parent Families: Development of a Predictive Model," *Journal of Divorce and Remarriage* 37 (2002): 13-36.

117 Wendy D. Manning, et al., "The Complexity of Fathers' Parenting Responsibilities and Involvement With Nonresident Children," *Journal of Family Issues* 24 (July 2003): 645-667.

118 Frank F. Furstenberg, Jr. and Julien O. Teitler, "Reconsidering the Effects of Marital Disruption," *Journal of Family Issues* 15 (June 1994): 173-190.

119 Timothy J. Biblarz and Greg Gottainer, "Family Structure and Children's Success: A Comparison of Widowed and Divorced Single-Mother Families," *Journal of Marriage and the Family* 62 (May 2000): 533-548.

120 Jay D. Teachman, "The Childhood Living Arrangements of Children and the Characteristics of Their Marriages," *Journal of Family Issues* 25 (January 2004): 86-111.

121 K. E. Kiernan and J. Hobcraft, "Parental Divorce During Childhood: Age at First Intercourse, Partnership and Parenthood," *Population Studies* 51 (1997): 41-55, as cited in *Family Planning Perspectives* 29 (September/October 1997): 240-242.

122 Jay Teachman, "Childhood Living Arrangements and the Formation of Coresidential Unions," *Journal of Marriage and Family* 65 (August 2003): 507-524.

123 Carole Mulder and Marjorie Lindner Gunnoe, "College Students' Attitudes Toward Divorce Based on Gender, Parental Divorce, and Parental Relationships," *Journal of Divorce & Remarriage* 31 (1999): 179-188.

124 Heather E. Sprague and Jennifer M. Kinney, "The Effects of Interparental Divorce and Conflict on College Students' Romantic Relationships," *Journal of Divorce and Remarriage* 27 (1997): 85-104.

125 William Axinn and Arland Thornton, "The Influence of Parents' Marital Dissolutions on Children's Attitudes Toward Family Formation," *Demography* 33 (February 1996): 66-81.

126 Teresa M. Cooney and Jane Kurz, "Mental Health Outcomes Following Recent Parental Divorce: The Case of Young Adult Offspring," *Journal of Family Issues* 17 (July 1996): 495-513.

127 Teresa M. Cooney, "Young Adults' Relations with Parents: The Influence of Recent Parental Divorce," *Journal of Marriage and the Family* 56 (February 1994): 45-56.

128 Ibid.

129 Andrew J. Cherlin, et al., "Effects of Parental Divorce on Mental Health Throughout the Life Course," *American Sociological Review* 63 (April 1998): 239-249.

130 Paul R. Amato and Juliana Sobolewski, "The Effects of Divorce and Marital Discord on Adult Children's Psychological Well-Being," *American Sociological Review* 66 (December 2001): 900-921.

131 Stephen E. Gilman and Ichiro Kawachi, et al., "Family Disruption in Childhood and Risk of Adult Depression," *American Journal of Psychiatry* 160 (May 2003): 939-946.

132 Shanta R. Dube, Robert F. Anda, et al., "Childhood Abuse, Household Dysfunction, and the Risk of Attempted Suicide Throughout the Life Span: Findings From the Adverse Childhood Experiences Study," *Journal of the American Medical Association* 286 (December 26, 2001): 3089-3096.

133 Paul R. Amato, "Explaining the Intergenerational Transmission of Divorce," *Journal of Marriage and the Family* 58 (August 1996): 628-640.

134 Paul R. Amato and Danelle D. DeBoer, "The Transmission of Marital Instability Across Generations: Relationship Skills or Commitment to Marriage?" *Journal of Marriage and Family* 63 (November 2001): 1038-1051.

135 Du Feng, et al., "Intergenerational Transmission of Marital Quality and Marital Instability," *Journal of Marriage and the Family* 61 (May 1999): 451-463.

136 Mary Ann Powell and Toby L. Parcel, "Effects of Family Structure on the Earnings Attainment Process: Differences by Gender," *Journal of Marriage and the Family* 59 (May 1997): 419-433.

137 Timothy J. Biblarz and Greg Gottainer, "Family Structure and Children's Success."

138 Diane Lye, et al., "Childhood Living Arrangements and Adult Children's Relations with Their Parents," *Demography* 32 (May 1995): 261-280.

139 Lilana Pezzin and Barbara Steinberg Schone, "Parental Marital Disruption and Intergenerational Transfers: An Analysis of Lone Elderly Parents and Their Children," *Demography* 36 (August 1999): 287-297.

140 Frederick O. Lorenz, et al., "Married and Recently Divorced Mothers' Stressful Events and Distress: Tracing Change Across Time," *Journal of Marriage and the Family* 59 (February 1997): 219-232.

141 Jennifer E. Lansford and Rosario Ceballo, et al., "Does Family Structure Matter? A Comparison of Adoptive, Two-Parent Biological, Single-Mother, Stepfather and Stepmother Households," *Journal of Marriage and Family* 63 (August 2001): 840-851.

142 Adam Shapiro and James David Lambert, "Longitudinal Effects of Divorce on the Quality of the Father-Child Relationship and on Fathers' Psychological Well-Being," *Journal of Marriage and the Family* 61 (May 1999): 397-408.

143 Robin W. Simon, "Revisiting the Relationships Among Gender, Marital Status and Mental Health," *American Journal of Sociology* 107 (January 2002): 1065-1096.

144 Amy Mehraban Pienta, "Health Consequences of Marriage for the Retirement Years," *Journal of Family Issues* 21 (July 2000): 559-586.

145 Augustine J. Kposowa, "Marital Status and Suicide in the National Longitudinal Mortality Study," *Journal of Epidemiology and Community Health* 54 (April 2000): 254-261.

146 Timothy J. Biblarz and Greg Gottainer, "Family Structure and Children's Success."

147 Sara McLanahan and Gary Sandefur, *Growing Up with a Single Parent: What Hurts, What Helps* (Cambridge: Harvard University Press, 1994), p. 24.

148 Pamela J. Smock, "The Economic Costs of Marital Disruption for Young Women Over the Past Two Decades," *Demography* 30 (August 1993): 353-371.

149 National Center for Health Statistics, *Cohabitation, Marriage, Divorce, and Remarriage in the United States*, Table 37.

150 Ibid., Table 41.

151 Hart and Teeter Research for NBC News, *Wall Street Journal*, June 16 – 19, 1999.

152 *Time*, CNN poll, May 7-8, 1997 as cited in Walter Kirn, "The Ties That Bind: Should Breaking Up Be Harder to Do? The Debate Over Easy Divorce Rages On," *Time*, August 18, 1997, p. 49.

153 Yankelovich Partners for *Time*, CNN, September 6-7, 2000 as cited in Walter Kirn, "Should You Stay Together for the Kids?" *Time*, September 25, 2000, p. 77.

154 Ibid.

155 General Social Survey, National Opinion Research Center, February 6 – June 26, 2002.

156 *Time*, CNN poll, May 7-8, 1997, as cited in Walter Kirn, "The Ties That Bind," p. 49.

157 Wirthlin Worldwide for the Alliance for Marriage, July 7-10, 2000.

CHAPTER 9 Single-Parent Families

158 U.S. Census Bureau, "Living Arrangements of Children Under 18 Years Old: 1960 to Present," Table CH-1, June 12, 2003.

159 Jason Fields, *Living Arrangements of Children 1996*, U.S. Census Bureau, Internet Table 2 and U.S. Census Bureau, "Living Arrangements of Children Under 18 Years Old: 1960 to Present."

160 U.S. Census Bureau, "Living Arrangements of Children Under 18 Years Old: 1960 to Present."

161 U.S. Census Bureau, "Children Under 18 Years Living With Mother Only, by Marital Status of Mother: 1960 to Present," Table CH-5, June 12, 2003. Percent calculations by the author.

162 Allen Dupree and Wendell Primus, "Declining Share of Children Lived With Single Mothers in the Late 1990s," Center on Budget and Policy Priorities, Washington, D.C., June 15, 2001, p. 1.

163 Ibid.

164 U.S. Census Bureau, "Children Under 18 Years Living With Father Only, by Marital Status of Father," Table CH-6, June 12, 2003. Percent calculations by the author.

165 Pat Fagan, "How Broken Families Rob Children of Their Chances for Future Prosperity," *Heritage Backgrounder* No. 1283, The Heritage Foundation, June 11, 1999, p. 13.

166 U.S. Bureau of the Census, "Historical Poverty Tables," Table 4, Available at *www.census.gov/hhes/poverty/histpov/hstpov4.html*.

167 Ibid.

168 Robert I. Lerman, "How Do Marriage, Cohabitation and Single Parenthood Affect the Material Hardships of Families with Children?"

169 Suet-Ling Pong, et al., "Family Policies and Children's School Achievement in Single- Versus Two-Parent Families," *Journal of Marriage and Family* 65 (August 2003): 681-699.

170 Jay Teachman, et al., "Sibling Resemblance in Behavioral and Cognitive Outcomes: The Role of Father Presence," *Journal of Marriage and the Family* 60 (November 1998): 835-848.

171 Gunilla Ringback Weitoft, et al., "Mortality, Severe Morbidity and Injury in Children Living with Single Parents in Sweden: A Population-based Study," *The Lancet* 361 (January 25, 2003): 289-295.

172 Dawn Upchurch, et al., "Gender and Ethnic Differences in the Timing of First Sexual Intercourse," *Family Planning Perspectives* 30 (May/June 1998): 121-127.

173 Jeanne M. Hilton and Esther L. Devall, "Comparison of Parenting and Children's Behavior in Single-Mother, Single-Father, and Intact Families," *Journal of Divorce and Remarriage* 29 (1998): 23-54.

174 Kelly J. Kelleher, et al., "Increasing Identification of Psychosocial Problems: 1979-1996," *Pediatrics* 105 (June 2000): 1313-1321.

175 Jocelyn Brown, et al., "A Longitudinal Analysis of Risk Factors for Child Maltreatment: Findings of a 17-Year Prospective Study of Officially Recorded and Self-Reported Child Abuse and Neglect," *Child Abuse & Neglect* 22 (1998): 1065-1078.

176 Andrea J. Sedlak and Diane D. Broadhurst, *The Third National Incidence Study of Child Abuse and Neglect*, U.S. Department of Health and Human Services, 1996, p. xviii.

177 Anne K. Driscoll, et al., "Nonmarital Childbearing Among Adult Women."

178 E. Michael Foster and Damon Jones, et al., "The Economic Impact of Nonmarital Childbearing: How Are Older, Single Mothers Faring?" *Journal of Marriage and the Family* 60 (February 1998): 163-174.

179 U.S. Census Bureau, "Historical Income Tables – Families," Table F-10, Available at *www.census.gov/hhes/income/histinc/f10.html.*

180 John Cairney and Michael Boyle, et al., "Stress, Social Support and Depression in Single and Married Mothers," *Social Psychiatry and Psychiatric Epidemiology* 38 (August 2003): 442-449.

181 Lorraine Davies, et al., "Significant Life Experiences and Depression Among Single and Married Mothers," *Journal of Marriage and the Family* 59 (May 1997): 294-308.

182 Steven Nock, "The Consequences of Premarital Fatherhood," *American Sociological Review* 63, (1998): 250-263, as cited in *Family Planning Perspectives* 30 (September/October 1998): 248-249.

183 U.S. Census Bureau, "Historical Income Tables – Families," Table F-10.

184 Wendy D. Manning, et al., "The Complexity of Fathers' Parenting Responsibilities and Involvement With Nonresident Children."

185 The Roper Center at the University of Connecticut, March 1997, Available at *www.publicagenda.org/issues/pcc_detail.cfm?issue_type=family&list=13.*

186 Steve Farkas, et al., "A Lot Easier Said Than Done: Parents Talk about Raising Children in Today's America," Public Agenda, 2002, p. 32.

187 Full question: "(I'm going to read a list of things that some people consider to be problems facing American families today. For each one, please tell me how serious a problem you feel it is for families today—very serious, fairly serious, just somewhat serious, or not much of a problem at all.)… The rise of single-parent households." Hart and Teeter Research Companies for NBC News, *Wall Street Journal*, June 16 – 19, 1999.

188 *New York Times* Poll, July 17-19, 1999.

189 Public Agenda, *Kids These Days '99: What Americans Think About the Next Generation Survey*, December 1-8, 1999.

190   International Communications Research for National Public Radio, Henry J. Kaiser
Family Foundation, Kennedy School, "Poverty in America Survey," January 4 –
February 27, 2001.

CHAPTER 10 Stepfamilies

191   According to the Census Bureau, only children of a householder (someone who
owns or rents the home) who were living in the household at the time of the
Census were counted; thus, there may have been other children in the household
who were not counted. "Census 2000 may have identified only about two-thirds of
all stepchildren living with at least one stepparent because of the manner in which
the data were collected." Rose M. Kreider, "Adopted Children and Stepchildren:
2000," *Census 2000 Special Reports*, U.S. Census Bureau, Washington, DC, p. 2.

192   James H. Bray and John Kelly, *Stepfamilies: Love, Marriage, and Parenting in the First
Decade* (New York: Broadway Books, 1998), p. 3, 11.

193   Larry L. Bumpass, et al., "The Changing Character of Stepfamilies."

194   Jennifer E. Lansford and Rosario Ceballo, et al., "Does Family Structure Matter? A
Comparison of Adoptive, Two-Parent Biological, Single-Mother, Stepfather and
Stepmother Households."

195   Frank W. Putnam, "Ten-Year Research Update Review: Child Sexual Abuse," *Journal
of the American Academy of Child and Adolescent Psychiatry* 42 (March 2003): 269-278.

196   Jean Giles-Sims, "Current Knowledge About Child Abuse in Stepfamilies," *Marriage
& Family Review* 25 (March/April 1997): 215-229.

197   Jocelyn Brown, et al., "A Longitudinal Analysis of Risk Factors for Child
Maltreatment: Findings of a 17-Year Prospective Study of Officially Recorded and
Self-Reported Child Abuse and Neglect."

198   William H. Jeynes, "Effects of Remarriage Following Divorce on the Academic
Achievement of Children," *Journal of Youth and Adolescence* 28 (June 1999): 385-393.

199   Nicholas Zill, "Understanding Why Children in Stepfamilies Have More Learning
and Behavior Problems Than Children in Nuclear Families," in Alan Booth and
Judy Dunn, eds. *Stepfamilies: Who Benefits? Who Does Not?* (Hillsdale, New Jersey:
Lawrence Erlbaum Associates, 1994), pp. 99-100.

200   Frances K. Goldscheider and Calvin Goldscheider, "The Effects of Childhood
Structure on Leaving and Returning Home," *Journal of Marriage and the Family* 60
(1998): 745-756.

201   John P. Hoffman and Robert A. Johnson, "A National Portrait of Family Structure
and Adolescent Drug Use," *Journal of Marriage and the Family* 60 (1998): 633-645.

202   Jeanne E. Jenkins and Sabina T. Zunguze, "The Relationship of Family Structure to
Adolescent Drug Use, Peer Affiliation, and Perception of Peer Acceptance of Drug
Use," *Adolescence* 33 (Winter 1998): 811-822.

203   Paula L. Antognoli-Toland, "Parent-Child Relationships, Family Structure and
Loneliness Among Adolescents," *Adolescent & Family Health* 2 (Spring 2001): 20-26.

204   David Popenoe, "The Evolution of Marriage and the Problem of Stepfamilies: A
Biosocial Perspective," *Stepfamilies: Who Benefits? Who Does Not?* p. 5.

205   Wendy D. Manning and Kathleen A. Lamb, "Adolescent Well-Being in Cohabiting, Married, and Single-Parent Families," *Journal of Marriage and Family* 65 (November 2003): 876-893.

206   Sandra L. Hofferth and Kermyt G. Anderson, "Are All Dads Equal? Biology Versus Marriage as a Basis for Paternal Investment," *Journal of Marriage and Family* 65 (February 2003): 213-232.

207   Liliana Pezzin and Barbara Steinberg Schone, "Parental Marital Disruption and Intergenerational Transfers: An Analysis of Lone Elderly Parents and Their Children."

208   Nadine F. Marks, "Midlife Marital Status Differences in Social Support Relationships with Adult Children and Psychological Well-Being," *Journal of Family Issues* 16 (1995): 5-28.

209   Stacy J. Rogers and Lynn K. White, "Satisfaction with Parenting: The Role of Marital Happiness, Family Structure, and Parents' Gender," *Journal of Marriage and the Family* 60 (May 1998): 293-308.

210   William L. MacDonald and Alfred DeMaris, "Parenting Stepchildren and Biological Children: The Effects of Stepparent's Gender and New Biological Children," *Journal of Family Issues* 17 (January 1996): 5-25.

211   Princeton Survey Research Associates for Pew Research Center, March 14-26, 1997.

CHAPTER 11

Teen Sex

If a girl experiences the love of a father who places her well-being above his own and who acts as a natural protector, then the girl is likely to delay sexual relations until she finds such a man herself. If she is denied such fatherly love, then the girl is likely to try to seek it elsewhere—often inappropriately and often at very young ages.

—Wade F. Horn
The Washington Times
July 1, 1997

BY THE NUMBERS: TEEN SEX

SNAPSHOT 1
The percentage of teens who have had premarital sex declined during the 1990s.

- In 1991, 54 percent of high school students had engaged in sexual intercourse, compared to 47 percent in 2003.

Percent of High School Students Who Have Had Sex, 1991-2003

YEAR	PERCENT OF ALL STUDENTS WHO HAVE HAD SEX	PERCENT OF GIRLS WHO HAVE HAD SEX	PERCENT OF BOYS WHO HAVE HAD SEX
1991	54.1	50.8	57.4
1993	53.0	50.2	55.6
1995	53.1	52.1	54.0
1997	48.4	47.7	48.8
1999	49.9	47.7	52.2
2001	45.6	42.9	48.5
2003	46.7	45.3	48.0

Source: Centers for Disease Control [1]

- In 2003, 45 percent of high school girls had engaged in sex, compared to 51 percent in 1991. Among boys, 48 percent had engaged in sex in 2003, compared to 57 percent in 1991.

Percent of High School Students Who Have Had Sex, 1991 and 2003

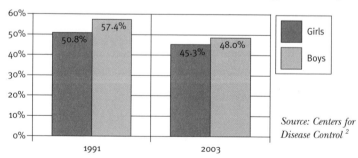

Source: Centers for Disease Control [2]

SNAPSHOT 2

The percentage of unwed girls who have had sex increased during the 1970s and 1980s before declining in the early 1990s.

Percent of Unwed Girls Age 15-19 Who Have Had Sex, 1971-1995

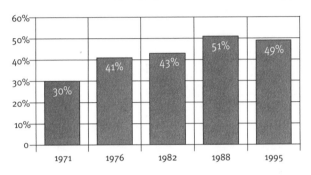

Source: National Center for Health Statistics [3]

SNAPSHOT 3

Older teens are more likely to have had premarital sex than are younger teens.

- In 2003, 33 percent of ninth graders reported having had sexual intercourse, compared to 62 percent of twelfth graders.

Percent of Teens Who Reported Having Had Sex, 2003

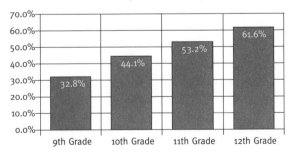

Source: Centers for Disease Control [4]

TEEN SEX: CAUSE & EFFECT

Teens who are raised by both parents from birth have lower probabilities of having sex ... than teens who grew up in any other family situation.

—Kristin Moore and Anne Driscoll
A Statistical Portrait of Adolescent Sex, Contraception and Childbearing

Family Background and Unwed Teen Sex

SNAPSHOT 1
Children who grow up with married parents are less likely to engage in premarital sex.

- A 2000 study of national data found that adolescents from single-parent families were more likely to have had sexual intercourse than were those living with both parents.[5]

- A 2002 study of 1,125 black men age 19-41 found that, compared to those raised in two-parent families, men raised by a single parent began having sex at an earlier age and had a higher lifetime number of sexual partners.[6]

- A 1998 UCLA study found that adolescents in single-parent families and stepfamilies were more likely to have had sexual intercourse and to be sexually active at an earlier age than were children who lived with both biological parents.[7]

- An analysis of data from the Adolescent Health Study shows that students in schools with a high prevalence of single-mother families are at 22 percent higher risk of early sexual intercourse than are students in schools with more two-parent families. Researchers attributed the correlation between single-parent families and early teen sex to a lack of "role modeling and collective supervision."[8]

SNAPSHOT 2

Teens' sexual behavior is influenced both by parental attitudes toward teen sex and by parental involvement in their lives.

- A 1997 longitudinal health study of 12,000 adolescents found that teens were more likely to delay sexual intercourse when they felt emotionally connected to their parents and when their parents disapproved of their being sexually active or of using contraception.[9]

- A 2001 study of over 3,500 students in grades 7-12 found that those who had more parental supervision, who felt cared for by their mother, and who perceived their mother's disapproval of premarital sex and birth control were less likely to engage in sexual activity.[10]

- A 2002 study of over 2,000 public high school students found that the greater amount of time youths spent unsupervised, the more likely they were to have had sex. Also, the more time boys were left unsupervised, the higher the number of lifetime sexual partners. Among those who had had sexual intercourse, "91 percent said that the last time had been in a home setting, including their own home (37 percent), their partner's home (43 percent), and a friend's home (12 percent), usually after school."[11]

THE CONSEQUENCES OF UNWED TEEN SEX

SNAPSHOT 1

Sexually transmitted diseases (STDs) are rampant among sexually active teens.

- Each year 3 million teens are infected with an STD.[12]

- About 25 percent of all new cases of STDs occur in teenagers; two-thirds of new cases occur in young people age 15-24.[13]

- In 2000, 48 percent of new STD cases (9.1 million) occurred among young people age 15-24; HPV, trichomoniasis and chlamydia accounted for 88 percent of new infections in this age group.[14]

- Gonorrhea rates are highest among 15- to 19-year-old females and 20- to 24-year-old males.[15]

- Teen girls have the highest rates of chlamydia infections; 46 percent of all reported infections occur among girls age 15-19, while 33 percent occur among 20- to 24-year-old women.[16]

- At least 10 percent of all sexually active teens are infected with pelvic inflammatory disease, a condition most often caused by untreated gonorrhea or chlamydia that can lead to infertility and ectopic pregnancy.[17]

- In 2000, the total direct medical cost for diagnosing and treating nine million new cases of STD's among young people age 15-24 was $6.5 billion, with HIV and HPV accounting for 90 percent of the total cost.[18]

SNAPSHOT 2
Teens who have premarital sex are likely to be promiscuous.

- A 2002 study of over 1,000 sexually experienced high school students found that among those who had sex before age 15, females were more than five times as likely, and males were 11 times more likely, to have multiple sexual partners than were those who delayed having sex.[19]

- A 2001 study found that adolescents who have sex at an early age are likely to engage in risky sexual behavior in later adolescence. Compared to other sexually experienced 10th graders, those who had sex in seventh grade were more than twice as likely to have had four or more sexual partners, twice as likely to have been pregnant or to have fathered a child and two-and-a-half times as likely to have forced someone to have sex.[20]

- A 2002 study of 1,125 adult black men found that those who began having sex at an early age had a higher lifetime number of sexual partners than did those who had their first sex at an older age.[21]

SNAPSHOT 3
Teens who engage in premarital sex are likely to suffer negative emotional consequences.

- Teens who engage in premarital sex are likely to experience regret, guilt, lowered self-respect, fear of commitment, depression and fears about pregnancy and STDs.[22]

- An analysis of data from a nationwide survey of adolescents found that, compared to girls who remain abstinent, sexually active girls are over three times more likely to be depressed and nearly three times more likely to attempt suicide. Sexually active teen boys are twice as likely to be depressed and eight times more likely to attempt suicide than are boys who remain abstinent.[23]

WHAT THE POLLS SAY ABOUT UNWED TEEN SEX

Adult Attitudes

SNAPSHOT 1
American adults strongly disapprove of young teens having

premarital sex, and parents are concerned about raising their teens in a sexually permissive society.

- In 2002, 71 percent of adults surveyed said that it is always wrong for young teens to have premarital sex.

Question: "What if they are in their early teens, say 14 to 16 years old? In that case, do you think sex relations before marriage are always wrong, almost always wrong, wrong only sometimes, or not wrong at all?"

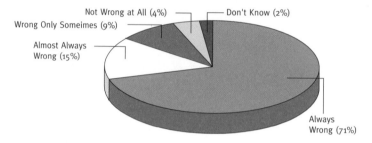

Source: General Social Survey [24]

- In 2000, 72 percent of parents of teens said they are very concerned about raising their teens in a sexually permissive society.

Question: "As I read a list of concerns about growing up today, please tell me how concerned you are about each aspect of raising teens today. What about . . . sexual permissiveness in society? Does this worry you a lot, a little, or not at all?"

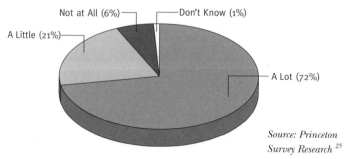

Source: Princeton Survey Research [25]

SNAPSHOT 2
Most Americans believe that parents should be notified before contraceptives are given to their daughters.

Question: "Currently, health clinics receiving money from the federal government distribute contraception to girls under the age of 18 without first notifying their parents. Do you think parents should have the right to know before their daughters under age 18 are given contraceptive drugs and/or devices?"

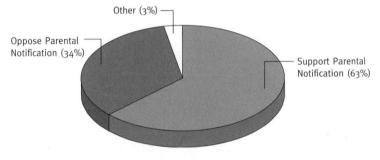

Source: The Polling Company [26]

SNAPSHOT 3
The majority of parents support the teaching of abstinence education.

- In a 2004 poll, 96 percent of parents said sex-ed classes should teach that abstinence from sexual activity is best for teens.

Question: "Assuming that a high school has sex-ed classes, please tell me do you strongly agree, somewhat agree, somewhat disagree or strongly disagree that the class should teach the following to teen students: abstinence from sexual activity is best for teens."

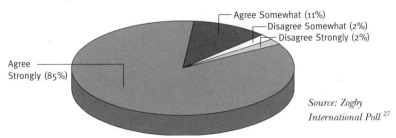

Source: Zogby International Poll [27]

- In 2004, 91 percent of parents said sex-ed classes should teach that the best choice is for sexual activity to be linked to love, intimacy and commitment—qualities most likely to occur in a faithful marriage.

Question:"Assuming that a high school has sex-ed classes, please tell me do you strongly agree, somewhat agree, somewhat disagree or strongly disagree that the class should teach the following to teen students: The best choice is for sexual intercourse to be linked to love, intimacy, and commitment. These qualities are most likely to occur in a faithful marriage."

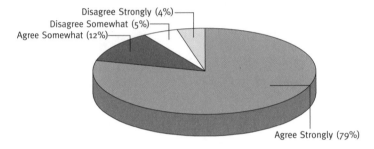

Disagree Strongly (4%)
Disagree Somewhat (5%)
Agree Somewhat (12%)
Agree Strongly (79%)

Source: Zogby International Poll [28]

Teen Attitudes

SNAPSHOT 1
Teens highly value sexual abstinence.

- Nearly all teenagers believe that teens should be given a strong message from society to abstain from sex until at least after high school.

Question: "How important do you think it is for teens to be given a strong message from society that they should abstain from sex until they are at least out of high school?"

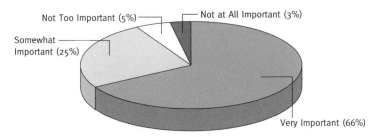

Not Too Important (5%) ── ── Not at All Important (3%)

Somewhat ── Important (25%)

Very Important (66%)

Source: International Communications Research [29]

- In 2000, 64 percent of teen girls surveyed said sexual activity is not acceptable for high-school age adolescents, even if precautions are taken to prevent pregnancy and sexually transmitted diseases. Fifty-three percent of teen boys agreed.

Question: "Some people think it is basically acceptable for high school-age teens to be sexually active, as long as they take steps to prevent pregnancy and STDs, including AIDS. Others do not think it is acceptable for high school-age teenagers to be sexually active whether they take precautions or not. Which comes closer to your view, the first statement or the second?"

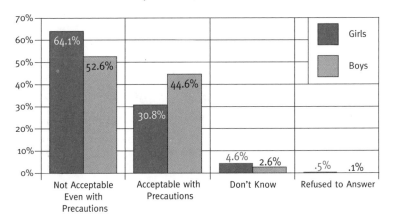

Girls

Boys

	Not Acceptable Even with Precautions	Acceptable with Precautions	Don't Know	Refused to Answer
Girls	64.1%	30.8%	4.6%	.5%
Boys	52.6%	44.6%	2.6%	.1%

Source: International Communications Research [30]

- In 2003, 73 percent of teens surveyed said they are not embarrassed to admit they are virgins.

Question: "Do you think it is embarrassing for teens to admit they are virgins?"

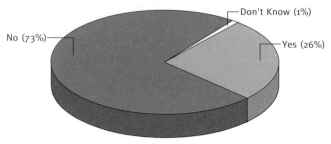

Source: International Communications Research [31]

- In 2003, 67 percent of sexually active teens said they wish they had waited longer to become sexually active.[32]

- In a 2003 survey, 92 percent of teens age 15-17 agreed that "being a virgin in high school is a good thing."[33]

SNAPSHOT 2
Teens' approval of premarital sex declined in the 1990s.

- In 1988, 73 percent of males age 15-19 said it was all right to have premarital sex even if a couple was not planning to get married, compared to 65 percent in 1995. In 1988, 11 percent said premarital sex was never all right until marriage, compared to 17 percent in 1995.[34]

- A 2001 nationwide survey found that 42 percent of college freshmen said it's alright to have casual sex, compared to 50 percent in 1990.

Question: "If two people really like each other, is it alright for them to have sex even if they've known each other for only a very short time?"

YEAR	PERCENT APPROVING OF CASUAL SEX	
2001	42.2%	*Source:* *The American Freshmen Survey* [35]
1990	50.1%	

SNAPSHOT 3

Teens say parents, friends, and religious/moral values most strongly influence their decisions about sex.

- In 2003, 45 percent of teens said their parents influenced their decisions about sex most strongly, while 31 percent said their friends influenced them most strongly.

Question: "When it comes to your decisions about sex, who is most influential?"

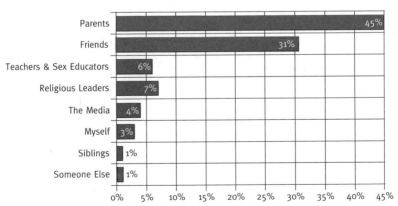

Source: International Communications Research [36]

CHAPTER 12

Teen Unwed Childbearing

The U.S. teen pregnancy rate is more than twice as high as that in any other advanced country and almost 10 times as high as the rate in Japan or the Netherlands.

—Rebecca Maynard
Kids Having Kids: Economic Costs and Social Consequences of Teen Pregnancy

BY THE NUMBERS: TEEN UNWED CHILDBEARING

SNAPSHOT 1
Four out of five births to teen girls occur outside marriage.

- In 2002, 80 percent of births to girls age 15-19 were out of wedlock.

Percentage of Births to Girls Age 15-19 that Were Out of Wedlock, 2002

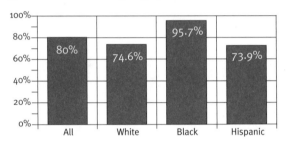

Percentage of Births to Girls Age 15-19 that Were Out of Wedlock, Historical

YEAR	ALL RACES	WHITE	BLACK	HISPANIC
1940	13.5%	7.0%	N/A	N/A
1950	13.4%	6.2%	N/A	N/A
1955	14.2%	6.4%	N/A	N/A
1960	14.8%	7.2%	N/A	N/A
1965	20.8%	11.4%	N/A	N/A
1969	27.8%	16.2%	58.7%	N/A
1970	29.5%	17.1%	62.7%	N/A
1975	38.2%	22.9%	76.9%	N/A
1980	47.6%	33.1%	85.7%	N/A
1985	58.0%	44.8%	90.2%	N/A
1987	63.4%	51.4%	91.4%	N/A
1990	67.1%	56.4%	92.0%	59.4%
1993	71.3%	62.3%	92.9%	62.8%
1995	75.2%	67.7%	95.2%	67.3%
1997	77.8%	71.1%	95.7%	71.6%
1999	78.6%	72.6%	95.5%	72.9%
2000	78.8%	72.8%	95.6%	72.6%
2002	80.0%	74.6%	95.7%	73.9%

Source: National Center for Health Statistics [37]

SNAPSHOT 2
The unwed teen birthrate has more than doubled since 1960.

- Between 1960 and 1994, the annual birthrate per 1,000 unmarried girls age 15-19 tripled, declining slightly after 1994.

- Among unmarried girls age 15-19, the birthrate historically has been higher for 18- and 19-year-olds.

Birthrates for Unmarried Girls Age 15-19, Historical

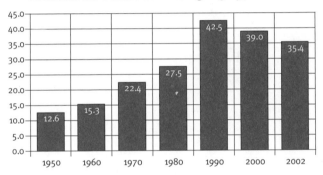

Year	Total, Age 15-19	Age 15-17	Age 18-19
1950	12.6	N/A	N/A
1960	15.3	N/A	N/A
1965	16.7	N/A	N/A
1970	22.4	17.1	32.9
1975	23.9	19.3	32.5
1980	27.5	20.7	38.7
1985	31.4	22.4	45.9
1990	42.5	29.6	60.7
1991	44.6	30.8	65.4
1992	44.2	30.2	66.7
1993	44.0	30.3	66.1
1994	45.8	31.7	69.1
1995	43.8	30.1	66.5
1996	42.2	28.5	64.9
1997	41.4	27.7	63.9
1998	40.9	26.5	63.7
1999	39.7	25.0	62.4
2000	39.0	23.9	62.2
2001	37.0	22.0	60.6
2002	35.4	20.8	58.6

Note: Birthrate is the annual number of births per 1,000 unmarried girls age 15-19.

Source: National Center for Health Statistics [38]

SNAPSHOT 3
Teen birthrates declined in the 1990s.

- In 2002, the birthrate per thousand unmarried 15- to 19-year-old girls was 22 births for whites, 66 for Hispanics and 65 for blacks.

- Among unmarried black teens, the birthrate peaked at 108 per thousand in 1991 and declined to 65 in 2002.

Birthrates among Unmarried Girls Age 15-19, 1990-2002

YEAR	TOTAL, ALL RACES	WHITE	BLACK	HISPANIC
1990	42.5	25.0	106.0	65.9
1991	44.6	N/A	107.8	71.0
1992	44.2	N/A	104.8	70.3
1993	44.0	N/A	101.2	71.1
1994	45.8	28.1	99.3	77.6
1995	43.8	27.7	91.2	73.2
1996	42.2	27.0	87.5	69.3
1997	41.4	26.4	84.5	69.2
1998	40.9	26.2	81.5	69.3
1999	39.7	25.6	76.5	68.6
2000	39.0	24.7	75.0	68.5
2001	37.0	23.1	69.9	67.1
2002	35.4	22.1	64.8	66.1

Note: Birthrate is the annual number of births per 1,000 unmarried girls age 15-19.
Source: National Center for Health Statistics [39]

- According to a 2003 study, the decline in unwed birthrates among 15- to 19-year-old girls between 1991 and 1995 was due to an increase in the number of abstinent teens.[40]

SNAPSHOT 4
The District of Columbia has a higher teen birthrate than any of the 50 states.

- In 2002, the District of Columbia had the highest teen birthrate, while New Hampshire had the lowest rate. The U.S. average was 43.0 births per thousand teenage girls.

State-by-State Teen Birthrates, 2002

STATE	BIRTHRATE	STATE	BIRTHRATE
District of Columbia	69.1	Nebraska	37.0
Mississippi	64.7	Oregon	36.8
Texas	64.4	Utah	36.8
New Mexico	62.4	Montana	36.4
Arizona	61.2	Rhode Island	35.6
Arkansas	59.9	Maryland	35.4
Louisiana	58.1	Michigan	34.8
Oklahoma	58.0	Washington	33.0
Georgia	55.7	Iowa	32.5
Alabama	54.5	Wisconsin	32.3
Tennessee	54.3	Pennsylvania	31.6
Nevada	53.9	New York	29.5
South Carolina	53.0	Minnesota	27.5
North Carolina	52.2	North Dakota	27.2
Kentucky	51.0	New Jersey	26.8
Colorado	47.0	Connecticut	25.8
Delaware	46.3	Maine	25.4
West Virginia	45.5	Vermont	24.2
Indiana	44.6	Massachusetts	23.3
Florida	44.5	New Hampshire	20.0
Missouri	44.1		
Kansas	43.0		
Illinois	42.2		
California	41.1		
Wyoming	39.9		
Alaska	39.5		
Ohio	39.5		
Idaho	39.1		
Hawaii	38.2		
South Dakota	38.0		
Virginia	37.6		

Note: Birthrate is the annual number of births per 1,000 unmarried girls age 15-19.
Source: National Center for Health Statistics [41]

TEEN UNWED CHILDBEARING: CAUSE & EFFECT

Family Background and Teen Unwed Childbearing

SNAPSHOT 1
Teens not raised in intact families are more likely to have children outside of marriage.

- A 1994 national study found that girls who lived in a single-parent household for some part of their childhood were twice as likely to give birth before age 20.[42]

- A 1998 study found that girls who lived with their married biological parents in eighth grade were only one-third as likely to have a premarital birth by grade 12 than were girls living in other family structures.[43]

- Researchers who followed American and New Zealand girls from age 5 until approximately age 18 found that pregnancy rates among American girls whose father was absent at an early age were 5 times higher (3 times higher for New Zealand) than were those among girls whose father was present, even after controlling for factors such as race, socioeconomic status, and marital conflict.[44]

- A 2000 study of teen mothers found that those who did not live with both biological parents in the eighth grade were at high risk for having a second birth in their teen years.[45]

SNAPSHOT 2
Parental involvement and parental attitudes toward sex affect the likelihood of their children becoming pregnant outside marriage.

- A 2000 study of approximately 10,000 adolescents in grades

7-11 found that those who perceived their mother's disapproval of their engaging in sex and were satisfied with their maternal relationship were less likely to have sex and to become pregnant. Adolescents who did not perceive maternal disapproval of their engaging in sex were six times more likely to have sex and 3.5 times more likely to become pregnant.[46]

- A 2003 study of 976 students in grades 7-12 found that those who felt more connected to their parents were much less likely to be sexually experienced or to have been involved in a pregnancy than were those who did not feel close to their parents.[47]

THE CONSEQUENCES OF TEEN UNWED CHILDBEARING

SNAPSHOT 1
Teen mothers tend to fare poorly educationally and economically.

- Adolescent mothers frequently live in poverty or are dependent on welfare.[48]

- Only about 50 percent of teen mothers finish high school while they are adolescents or young adults.[49]

SNAPSHOT 2
Teen mothers are likely to remain single for most of their children's early years and to suffer emotionally.

- Most teenage mothers are unmarried five years after having a baby. Less than half of the teenagers who have children out of wedlock marry within ten years after giving birth.[50]

- Only 20 to 30 percent of the male partners of teen mothers marry their child's mother.[51]

- A 2002 study of 990 teen mothers found that those who had their first child out of wedlock experienced more symptoms of depression at age 27-29 than did mothers who were married when their first child was born. The researchers concluded that "virtually all of the effects of single teen motherhood on depressive symptoms in young adulthood were due to marital status, not age, at first birth."[52]

SNAPSHOT 3
Children of teen mothers compare unfavorably to other children on a variety of measurements.

- A 2001 study based on national data found that children born to teen mothers are more likely than other children to have low math and reading scores, to repeat a grade, to have sex before age 16, to fight at school or work, or to skip school.[53]

- A 1997 study of more than 50,000 adolescents found that those born to teenage or unmarried mothers were at a greater risk of juvenile delinquency than were those born to married mothers. Males from these families were 1.7 times more likely to become chronic offenders, while the females were 1.8 times more likely to be offenders and 2.8 times more likely to be chronic offenders.[54]

- Children of teen mothers are more likely to not graduate from high school, to be abused or neglected or to have a child as an unmarried teenager.[55]

- A 2002 study found that, compared to children born to adult mothers, those born to teen mothers are more likely to score lower on achievement tests and to have more aggressive behavior.[56]

SNAPSHOT 4
Teen childbearing creates high costs for society.

- Teenage childbearing costs U.S. taxpayers an estimated $7 billion annually for increased welfare, food stamps, medical, incarceration and foster care costs as well as lost tax revenue due to government dependency.[57]

- The gross annual cost to society of adolescent childbearing and its negative consequences is $29 billion, which includes the administration of welfare and foster care programs, the building and maintenance of additional prisons, lower educational achievement and reduced productivity among unwed parents.[58]

WHAT THE POLLS SAY ABOUT TEEN UNWED CHILDBEARING

Adult Attitudes

SNAPSHOT 1
Most Americans think unwed teen pregnancy is a serious problem.

- In 2003, 73 percent of adults said teen pregnancy is a major problem in the U.S.

Question: "I am going to read you a list of issues that teens today may face. For each one, please tell me how big a problem you think it is for teens in general—a major problem, a minor problem, or not a problem at all.... Unwanted pregnancy ..."

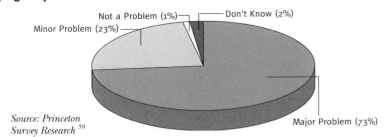

Not a Problem (1%)
Don't Know (2%)
Minor Problem (23%)
Major Problem (73%)

Source: Princeton Survey Research [59]

SNAPSHOT 2

Black and Hispanic adults are more likely than whites to say teen pregnancy is a major problem.

Question: "For each issue I read please tell me if you think it is a major problem facing our country, a minor problem, or not a problem at all ... teen pregnancy."

Percent Citing Teen Pregnancy as a "Major Problem"

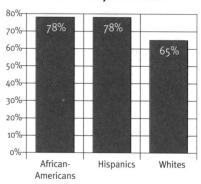

Source: Princeton Survey Research [60]

Teen Attitudes

SNAPSHOT 1

During the last 20 years, teens have grown more accepting of out-of-wedlock childbearing.

- In the late 1990s, 54 percent of high school senior girls said couples who have a child without being married are "experimenting with a worthwhile alternative lifestyle" or "doing their own thing and not affecting anyone else." Only 33 percent responded this way in the late 1970s.

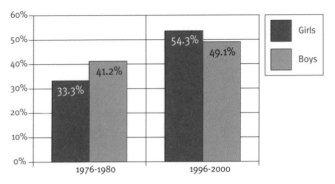

Percentage of High School Seniors Who Find Unwed Childbearing Acceptable, Historical

Years	Boys	Girls
1976-1980	41.2%	33.3%
1981-1985	43.2%	40.3%
1986-1990	46.6%	47.8%
1991-1995	49.1%	53.3%
1996-2000	49.1%	54.3%

Source: Monitoring the Future Study [61]

SNAPSHOT 2

The majority of teens think that teen pregnancy prevention programs should promote childbearing within marriage.

- In a 2003 survey, 83 percent of teens said teen pregnancy prevention programs should teach young people to be married before they have a child.

Question: "Do you agree or disagree with this statement: Teen pregnancy prevention programs should teach young people to be married before they have a child?"

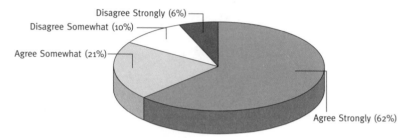

Disagree Strongly (6%)

Disagree Somewhat (10%)

Agree Somewhat (21%)

Agree Strongly (62%)

Source: International Communications Research [62]

CHAPTER 13

Teen Abortion

The greatest destroyer of peace today is abortion, because it is a war against the child—a direct killing of the innocent child—murder by the mother herself. And if we accept that a mother can kill even her own child, how can we tell other people not to kill one another?

—*Mother Theresa*
1994 National Prayer Breakfast

SNAPSHOT 1

Since 1973, 9.4 million abortions have been performed on women under age 20.[63]

- In 1999, 249,660 abortions were performed on women under age 20; 61 percent of these were performed on 18- and 19-year old women.

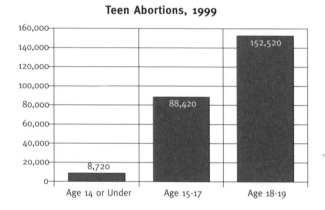

Teen Abortions, 1999

Teen Abortions, Historical

YEAR	AGE 14 OR UNDER	AGE 15-17	AGE 18-19
1972	N/A	86,140	104,860
1973	11,630	104,590	127,310
1975	15,260	140,520	186,260
1979	16,220	178,570	266,030
1980	15,340	183,350	261,430
1985	16,970	165,630	233,570
1990	12,580	129,820	221,150
1993	12,410	112,960	174,750
1995	10,830	105,970	156,960
1997	9,640	98,460	157,180
1999	8,720	88,420	152,520

Source: Alan Guttmacher Institute [64]

- Among women who have had abortions in the United States, 19 percent are teens, 33 percent are age 20-24 and 48 percent are age 25 and older.[65]

SNAPSHOT 2
In 1999, the District of Columbia had a higher teen abortion rate than any of the 50 states.

- Both New York and New Jersey had the highest teen abortion rates among the 50 states in 1999, while Utah had the lowest. The U.S. average was 25 abortions per thousand girls age 15-19.

State-by-State Teen Abortion Rates, 1999

STATE	ABORTION RATE	STATE	ABORTION RATE
District of Columbia	59	Alaska	17
New York	47	South Carolina	17
New Jersey	47	Alabama	16
Maryland	42	Montana	16
California	37	Tennessee	16
Nevada	36	Maine	15
Florida	35	Mississippi	15
Hawaii	35	New Hampshire	15
Connecticut	30	Missouri	14
Delaware	30	Nebraska	14
Oregon	27	Vermont	14
Washington	27	Arkansas	13
Illinois	25	Idaho	13
Massachusetts	25	Indiana	13
Michigan	25	Kansas	13
North Carolina	23	Minnesota	13
Rhode Island	23	Iowa	12
Virginia	22	Louisiana	12
Wyoming	22	Wisconsin	12
Arizona	21	Oklahoma	11
Colorado	21	Kentucky	10
Georgia	21	South Dakota	9
New Mexico	19	West Virginia	9
Texas	19	North Dakota	8
Ohio	18	Utah	6
Pennsylvania	18		

Rate is the annual number of abortions per 1,000 girls age 15-19.
Source: The Alan Guttmacher Institute [66]

WHAT THE POLLS SAY ABOUT ABORTION

SNAPSHOT 1

Approval of abortion among college freshmen in 2003 was much lower than it was a decade earlier.

- In 1991, 65 percent of college freshmen agreed that abortion should be legal, compared to 55 percent in 2003.

Question: "Do you agree or disagree, strongly or somewhat ... Abortion should be legal?"

Respondents Who Think Abortion Should Be Legal

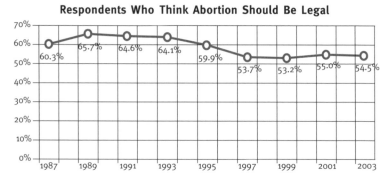

Source: American Freshman Survey [67]

- In 2003, 72 percent of teens age 13-17 said that abortion is morally wrong.

Question: "Regardless of whether or not you think it should be legal, for each one, please tell me whether you personally believe that in general it is morally acceptable or morally wrong. How about abortion?"

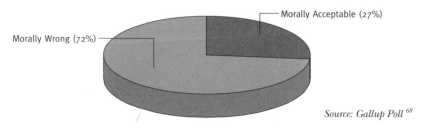

Morally Acceptable (27%)

Morally Wrong (72%)

Source: Gallup Poll [68]

SNAPSHOT 2

Male teens increasingly feel abortion on demand is an unacceptable practice.

- In 1988, 37 percent of male teens said it was all right for a female to have an abortion for any reason, compared to 24 percent in 1995.

Question: "When is it all right for a woman to have an abortion? . . . If the female wanted the abortion for any reason?"

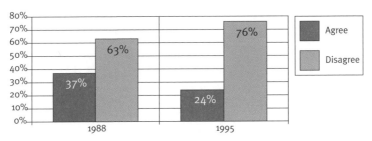

Source: National Survey of Adolescent Males [69]

CHAPTER 14

Teen Drug and Alcohol Abuse

Educate your child about the mental and physical harm [of drug and alcohol use], but also talk to him about right and wrong.... Youngsters who get hooked neglect school, grades, homework, and everyday responsibilities. In the end, they will neglect God, family, friends and character. When children use drugs and alcohol, they put at risk everything in their lives that is noble and worthwhile. If you arm children with that recognition, they stand a much better chance of holding firm against temptation.

William J. Bennett, Chester E. Finn, Jr.,
John T.E. Cribb, Jr.
The Educated Child

BY THE NUMBERS:
TEEN DRUG AND ALCOHOL ABUSE

SNAPSHOT 1
Teen drug use increased significantly during the 1990s.

- In 1991, 44 percent of high school seniors reported ever using illicit drugs, compared to 53 percent in 2002.

Percent of Students Who Reported Ever Using Illicit Drugs, 1991 and 2002

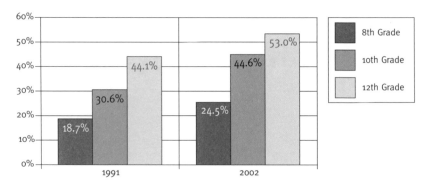

Percent of Students Who Reported Ever Using Illicit Drugs, 1991-2002

YEAR	8TH GRADE	10TH GRADE	12TH GRADE
1991	18.7%	30.6%	44.1%
1992	20.6%	29.8%	40.7%
1993	22.5%	32.8%	42.9%
1994	25.7%	37.4%	45.6%
1995	28.5%	40.9%	48.4%
1996	31.2%	45.4%	50.8%
1997	29.4%	47.3%	54.3%
1998	29.0%	44.9%	54.1%
1999	28.3%	46.2%	54.7%
2000	26.8%	45.6%	54.0%
2001	26.8%	45.6%	53.9%
2002	24.5%	44.6%	53.0%

*Source:
Monitoring the
Future* [70]

**See endnotes
for description of
drugs*

- Since 1997, the percentage of students using illicit drugs in the past 30 days has steadily decreased among eighth and tenth graders; among twelfth graders, this proportion has remained high.

Percent of Students Using Illicit Drugs in the Past 30 Days, 1991-2002

Year	8th Grade	10th Grade	12th Grade
1991	5.7%	11.6%	16.4%
1992	6.8%	11.0%	14.4%
1993	8.4%	14.0%	18.3%
1994	10.9%	18.5%	21.9%
1995	12.4%	20.2%	23.8%
1996	14.6%	23.2%	24.6%
1997	12.9%	23.0%	26.2%
1998	12.1%	21.5%	25.6%
1999	12.2%	22.1%	25.9%
2000	11.9%	22.5%	24.9%
2001	11.7%	22.7%	25.7%
2002	10.4%	20.8%	25.4%

Source: Monitoring the Future [71]

SNAPSHOT 2
More teens are reporting marijuana use.

- During the 1990s, the percentage of eighth graders who reported ever using marijuana nearly doubled.

- In 2002, 39 percent of 10th graders and 48 percent of 12th graders reported having tried marijuana.

Percent of Students Who Reported Ever Using Marijuana, 1991 and 2002

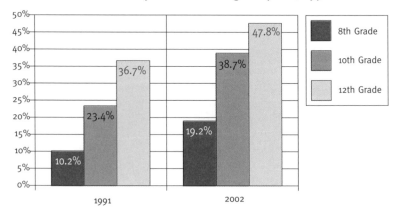

Percent of Students Who Reported Ever Using Marijuana, 1991-2002

Year	8th Grade	10th Grade	12th Grade
1991	10.2%	23.4%	36.7%
1992	11.2%	21.4%	32.6%
1993	12.6%	24.4%	35.3%
1994	16.7%	30.4%	38.2%
1995	19.9%	34.1%	41.7%
1996	23.1%	39.8%	44.9%
1997	22.6%	42.3%	49.6%
1998	22.2%	39.6%	49.1%
1999	22.0%	40.9%	49.7%
2000	20.3%	40.3%	48.8%
2002	19.2%	38.7%	47.8%

*Source:
Monitoring the
Future* [72]

- Daily use of marijuana among teens increased substantially during the 1990s: between 1991 and 2002, the percentage of students who used marijuana daily increased six-fold for eighth graders and three-fold for twelfth graders.

Percent of Students Using Marijuana Daily,* 1991-2002

YEARS	8TH GRADE	10TH GRADE	12TH GRADE
1991	0.2%	0.8%	2.0%
1992	0.2%	0.8%	1.9%
1993	0.4%	1.0%	2.4%
1994	0.7%	2.2%	3.6%
1995	0.8%	2.8%	4.6%
1996	1.5%	3.5%	4.9%
1997	1.1%	3.7%	5.8%
1998	1.1%	3.6%	5.6%
1999	1.4%	3.8%	6.0%
2000	1.3%	3.8%	6.0%
2001	1.3%	4.5%	5.8%
2002	1.2%	3.9%	6.0%

*Daily use is defined as using marijuana on 20 or more occasions in the past 30 days.

Source: Monitoring the Future [73]

SNAPSHOT 3
Underage drinking declined during the 1990s, but is still common.

- In 2002, 47 percent of eighth graders, 67 percent of tenth graders and 78 percent of twelfth graders had ever used alcohol.

Percent of Students Who Reported Ever Using Alcohol, 2002

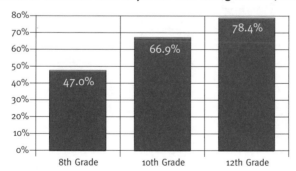

Percent of Students Who Reported Ever Using Alcohol, 1991-2002

Year	8th Grade	10th Grade	12th Grade
1991	70.1%	83.8%	88.0%
1992	69.3%	82.3%	87.5%
1993	67.1%	80.8%	87.0%
1994	55.8%	71.1%	80.4%
1995	54.5%	70.5%	80.7%
1996	55.3%	71.8%	79.2%
1997	53.8%	72.0%	81.7%
1998	52.5%	69.8%	81.4%
1999	52.1%	70.6%	80.0%
2000	51.7%	71.4%	80.3%
2001	50.5%	70.1%	79.7%
2002	47.0%	66.9%	78.4%

Source: Monitoring the Future [74]

- Among high school seniors in 2002, 72 percent had used alcohol in the past year and 49 percent had used it within 30 days of the survey.

Alcohol Use among High School Seniors, 1991-2002

Year	Lifetime	Past Year	Past 30 Days	Binge Drinking* Past Two Weeks
1991	88.0%	77.7%	54.0%	29.8%
1992	87.5%	76.8%	51.3%	27.9%
1993	87.0%	76.0%	48.6%	27.5%
1994	80.4%	73.0%	50.1%	28.2%
1995	80.7%	73.7%	51.3%	29.8%
1996	79.2%	72.5%	50.8%	30.2%
1997	81.7%	74.8%	52.7%	31.3%
1998	81.4%	74.3%	52.0%	31.5%
1999	80.0%	73.8%	51.0%	30.8%
2000	80.3%	73.2%	50.0%	30.0%
2001	79.7%	73.3%	49.8%	29.7%
2002	78.4%	71.5%	48.6%	28.6%

Five or more drinks in a row in the past two weeks.
Source: Monitoring the Future [75]

- In 2002, 44 percent of 10th graders and 62 percent of twelfth graders reported having been drunk at least once.

Percent of Students Who Had Ever Been Drunk, 2002

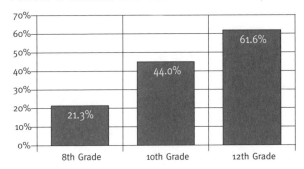

Percent of Students Who Had Ever Been Drunk, 1991-2002

YEAR	8TH GRADE	10TH GRADE	12TH GRADE
1991	26.7%	50.0%	65.4%
1992	26.8%	47.7%	63.4%
1993	26.4%	47.9%	62.5%
1994	25.9%	47.2%	62.9%
1995	25.3%	46.9%	63.2%
1996	26.8%	48.5%	61.8%
1997	25.2%	49.4%	64.2%
1998	24.8%	46.7%	62.4%
1999	24.8%	48.9%	62.3%
2000	25.1%	49.3%	62.3%
2001	23.4%	48.2%	63.9%
2002	21.3%	44.0%	61.6%

Source: Monitoring the Future [76]

TEEN DRUG AND ALCOHOL ABUSE: CAUSE & EFFECT

Family Background and Teen Drug and Alcohol Abuse

SNAPSHOT 1
Children in intact families are less likely to abuse alcohol and drugs.

- Interviews of more than 4,000 youth in 1999 revealed that, compared to those in intact families, those who had experienced one or more changes in family structure during adolescence were at much greater risk for drug abuse.[77]

- A 1998 study of fifth and sixth graders found that children from divorced homes reported more substance abuse than did children with married parents.[78]

- A 2003 study of 8,613 adults found that, compared to persons from intact families, those who experienced parental divorce are one-and-a-half times more likely to use illegal drugs by age 14 and two-thirds more likely to use illicit drugs at any age.[79]

- According to a Swedish study of almost a million children, children raised by single parents are more than twice as likely as those raised in two-parent homes to suffer from a serious psychiatric disorder, to commit or attempt suicide or to develop an alcohol addiction. Girls from single-parent homes are three times more likely to become addicted to drugs and boys are four times more likely.[80]

SNAPSHOT 2
Parental involvement helps prevent teen substance abuse.

- A 2002 study of over 2,000 public high school students found that the more time boys spent unsupervised, the more likely they were to use alcohol and tobacco. Both boys and girls who were unsupervised for more than 30 hours per week were much more likely to use marijuana than were those unsupervised for 5 hours or less.[81]

- According to a 2001 study of rural seventh and eighth graders, those who feel close to their parents are less likely to have used alcohol and drugs and more likely to have negative attitudes toward alcohol than are adolescents who did not experience close relationships with their parents.[82]

- A 2003 study found that the more often teens eat dinner with their family, the less likely they are to smoke, drink alcohol or use illegal drugs. Compared to teens who eat dinner with their parents twice a week or less, those who have family dinners five or more nights a week are 45 percent more likely to have never tried alcohol and 24 percent more likely to have never smoked marijuana.[83]

Consequences of Teen Drug and Alcohol Abuse

SNAPSHOT 1
Underage drinkers and marijuana users frequently develop substance dependence and more serious substance abuse problems.

- Youth who begin drinking before age 15 are four times more likely to develop alcohol dependence than are those who begin drinking as adults.[84]

- Marijuana dependence is a serious problem for youth: in 1996, 45 percent of those who sought treatment for marijuana were teenagers or younger. More teens are in treatment for marijuana use than for alcohol abuse, according to the National Center on Addiction and Substance Abuse.[85]

- A 2003 study of adult Australian twins found that those who used marijuana before age 17 were two to five times more likely to use other illicit drugs and to become dependent on alcohol or drugs than were their siblings who did not use marijuana by age 17.[86]

- A 2003 study of more than 11,700 college students from 128 colleges found that among those who drink, those who became drunk before age 13 were three times more likely to become alcohol dependent, twice as likely to report binge drinking, and twice as likely to have unplanned sex than were those who began drinking at age 19 or older.[87]

SNAPSHOT 2

Teen drug abuse and underage drinking are associated with academic problems.

- High school students who drink are five times more likely than their peers to drop out of school, and alcohol use is associated with 28 percent of all college dropouts, according to the National Clearinghouse for Alcohol and Drug Information.[88]

- A study of college drinking revealed that the heaviest drinkers get the lowest grades.[89]

- According to the National Institute on Drug Abuse, marijuana use can harm short-term memory, concentration and intellectual development. Students who use marijuana have lower grades and are less likely to graduate from high school than are those who do not smoke marijuana.[90]

SNAPSHOT 3
Teens who use alcohol and drugs are more likely to have pre-marital sex.

- In a 2002 survey, almost one-third of sexually active young people said they have "done more" sexually than they had planned while drinking or using drugs.[91]

- Teens who drink are twice as likely and teen drug users three times as likely to have had at least four sex partners than are their peers who do not drink or use drugs.[92]

SNAPSHOT 4
Youth substance abuse correlates with criminal behavior.

- Adolescents who use marijuana are at least three times more likely than their peers are to drive under the influence, to sell illegal drugs, or to commit theft, vandalism or battery.[93]

- A 2002 National Institute of Justice survey of ten cities found that about 60 percent of male juveniles who had been arrested tested positive for drugs, ranging from 51.6 percent in San Antonio to 72 percent in Phoenix.[94]

WHAT THE POLLS SAY ABOUT TEEN DRUG AND ALCOHOL ABUSE

Adult Attitudes

SNAPSHOT 1
Teen drug and alcohol abuse is a major concern for Americans.

- In a 2003 survey, 48 percent of adults said drug and alcohol use is the biggest problem facing teenagers today.

Question: "You said ... suicide, unwanted pregnancy, getting HIV/AIDS, poor academic performance, getting sexually transmitted diseases (other than HIV/AIDS), violence, use of alcohol or other illegal drugs were major problems for teens. Which one is the biggest problem?"

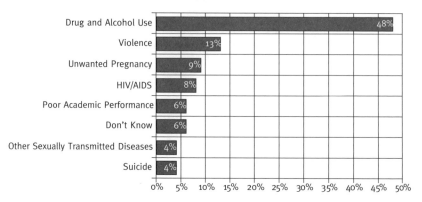

Source: Princeton Survey Research Associates [95]

SNAPSHOT 2

Americans think parents play a big role in determining whether a teen tries illegal drugs.

- In 2001, 79 percent of adults said parental supervision greatly affects whether or not a teenager tries illegal drugs.

Question: "Would you say ... lack of parental supervision ... is a major factor in whether a teenager tries illegal drugs, a minor factor, or not a factor at all?"

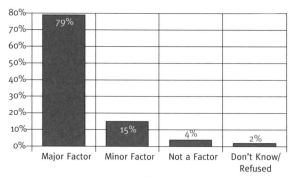

Source: Princeton Survey Research [96]

• In a 2003 survey, half of adults surveyed said parents are responsible for underage drinking.

Question: "Of the groups we just discussed, who would you say bears the most responsibility for underage drinking?"

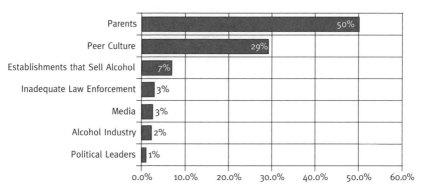

Source: *National Center on Addiction and Substance Abuse* [97]

Teen Attitudes

SNAPSHOT 1
Adolescent acceptance of marijuana use is on the rise.

• In 1991, 79 percent of 12th graders disapproved of occasional marijuana use, compared to 63 percent in 2002.

Question: "Do you disapprove of people who smoke marijuana occasionally?"

Percent of Students Who Disapprove of Occasional Marijuana Use, 1991 and 2002

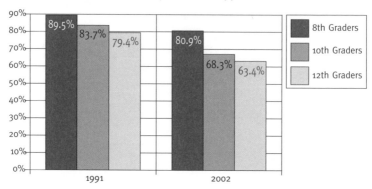

Percent of Students Who Disapprove of Occasional Marijuana Use, 1991-2002

YEAR	8TH GRADE	10TH GRADE	12TH GRADE
1991	89.5%	83.7%	79.4%
1992	88.1%	83.6%	79.7%
1993	85.7%	79.4%	75.5%
1994	80.9%	72.3%	68.9%
1995	79.7%	70.0%	66.7%
1996	76.5%	66.9%	62.9%
1997	78.1%	66.2%	63.2%
1998	78.4%	67.3%	64.4%
1999	79.3%	68.2%	62.5%
2000	80.6%	67.2%	65.8%
2001	80.6%	66.2%	63.2%
2002	80.9%	68.3%	63.4%

*12th graders were asked about people who are 18 years or older.

Source: Monitoring the Future [98]

- In 1991, 79 percent of high school seniors believed that there was a "great risk" of harm to adolescents who smoke marijuana regularly, compared to 53 percent in 2002.

Question: "How much do you think people risk harming themselves (physically or in other ways) if they smoke marijuana regularly?"

Percent Who Think Regular Marijuana Use Is Harmful, 1991 and 2002

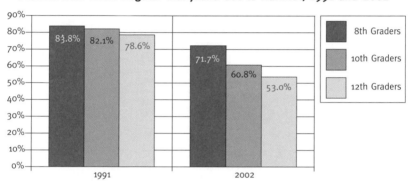

Percent Who Think Regular Marijuana Use Is Harmful, 1991-2002

Year	8th Grade	10th Grade	12th Grade
1991	83.8%	82.1%	78.6%
1992	82.0%	81.1%	76.5%
1993	79.6%	78.5%	72.5%
1994	74.3%	71.3%	65.0%
1995	73.0%	67.9%	60.8%
1996	70.9%	65.9%	59.9%
1997	72.7%	65.9%	58.1%
1998	73.0%	65.8%	58.5%
1999	73.3%	65.9%	57.4%
2000	74.8%	64.7%	58.3%
2001	72.2%	62.8%	57.4%
2002	71.7%	60.8%	53.0%

Source: Monitoring the Future [99]

SNAPSHOT 2

Older teens are more likely to approve of excessive drinking than are younger teens.

• In 2002, 82 percent of eighth graders disapproved of binge drinking, compared to 72 percent of tenth graders and 65 percent of twelfth graders.

Question: "Do you disapprove of people who have five or more drinks once or twice each weekend?"

Percent Who Disapprove of Binge Drinking, 1991-2002

YEAR	8TH GRADE	10TH GRADE	12TH GRADE
1991	85.2%	76.7%	67.4%
1992	83.9%	77.6%	70.7%
1993	83.3%	74.7%	70.1%
1994	80.7%	72.3%	65.1%
1995	80.7%	72.2%	66.7%
1996	79.1%	70.7%	64.7%
1997	81.3%	70.2%	65.0%
1998	81.0%	70.5%	63.8%
1999	80.3%	69.9%	62.7%
2000	81.2%	68.2%	65.2%
2001	81.6%	69.2%	62.9%
2002	81.9%	71.5%	64.7%

Source: Monitoring the Future [100]

CHAPTER 15

Juvenile Delinquency

From the wild Irish slums of the 19th century Eastern seaboard to the riot-torn suburbs of Los Angeles, there is one unmistakable lesson in American history: a community that allows a large number of young men to grow up in broken families, dominated by women, never acquiring any stable relationship to male authority, never acquiring any rational expectations about the future—that community asks for and gets chaos. Crime, violence, unrest, disorder—most particularly the furious, unrestrained lashing out at the whole structure—that is not only to be expected; it is very near to inevitable. And it is richly deserved.

—Sen. Daniel Patrick Moynihan
Family and the Nation

Despite the difficulty of proving causation in the social sciences, the weight of evidence increasingly supports the conclusion that fatherlessness is a primary generator of violence among young men.

—David Blankenhorn
Fatherless America [101]

BY THE NUMBERS: JUVENILE DELINQUENCY

SNAPSHOT 1
The juvenile arrest rate for violent crime increased dramatically between the 1960s and the 1990s.

- The overall juvenile arrest rate for violent crimes more than tripled from 1965 to 1992.

- Between 1965 and 1992, the juvenile violent crime arrest rate among white youth increased more than 400 percent. Among blacks, the increase was nearly 150 percent.

Juvenile Arrest Rates for Violent Crimes, 1965-1992

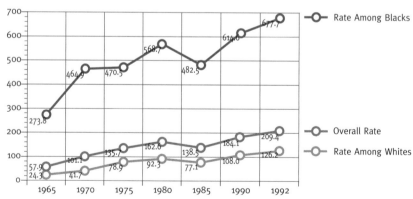

Source: U.S. Department of Justice [102]

Notes: *Violent crime includes murder, forcible rape, robbery and aggravated assault. Arrest rate is the annual number of arrests per 100,000 youth under age 18.*
*This measure was discontinued after 1992.

SNAPSHOT 2

Juvenile arrest rates peaked in the mid-1990s and since then have declined.

- The juvenile violent crime arrest rate reached its highest level ever in 1994, then dropped 44 percent by 2001 to its lowest level since 1983.

- The juvenile arrest rate for all crimes reached an all-time high in 1996, then declined 27 percent by 2001.

Juvenile Arrest Rates, 1990-2001

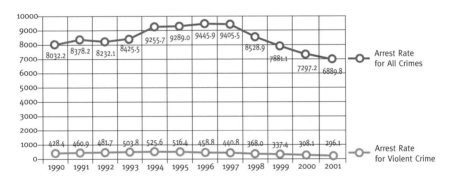

Notes: *Violent Crime Index includes murder, non-negligent manslaughter, forcible rape, robbery, and aggravated assault. Rate is the annual number of arrests per 100,000 youth age 10–17.*

Source: *Office of Juvenile Justice and Delinquency Prevention* [103]

SNAPSHOT 3

Among the 2.3 million arrests of juveniles in 2001, property crime was the most common offense.

MOST SERIOUS OFFENSE CHARGED	2001 JUVENILE ARREST ESTIMATES
Total	2,273,500
Property Crime Index	491,400
Other Assaults	239,000
Drug Abuse Violations	202,500
Disorderly Conduct	171,700
Liquor Law Violations	138,100
Vandalism	105,300
Violent Crime Index	96,500

Notes: Property Crime Index includes burglary, larceny-theft, motor vehicle theft, and arson. Violent Crime Index includes murder and non-negligent manslaughter, forcible rape, robbery, aggravated assault.

Source: Office of Juvenile Justice and Delinquency Prevention [104]

SNAPSHOT 5

Juvenile arrest rates for girls increased during the late 1980s and early 1990s.

- Between 1988 and 1994, female juvenile arrest rates for violent crimes nearly doubled, while the rates for property crimes increased by 31 percent. Among males, juvenile arrest rates for violent crimes increased 56 percent.

- From 1994 to 2001, juvenile arrest rates for property crimes declined 26 percent for females and 46 percent for males.

- Females accounted for 28 percent of all juvenile arrests in 2001.[105]

- In 2001, 59 percent of all juveniles arrested for running away from home were females.[106]

Juvenile Arrest Rates by Sex, 1980-2001

Year	Juvenile Arrest Rate for Property Crime Index Offenses		Juvenile Arrest Rate for Violent Crime Index Offenses	
	Males	Females	Males	Females
1980	4081.9	975.7	586.7	70.4
1985	3664.8	1012.5	527.7	67.1
1988	3750.6	1016.5	563.2	77.2
1990	3903.1	1151.7	735.7	104.6
1992	3784.5	1187.1	818.4	126.6
1994	3689.6	1327.7	879.0	152.6
1996	3367.8	1324.7	757.3	143.5
1998	2721.2	1137.4	593.9	129.5
2000	2183.9	1000.7	489.6	116.6
2001	1993.8	976.9	470.9	111.6

Note: Rates are the annual number of arrests per 100,000 youth age 10–17. The Property Crime Index includes burglary, larceny-theft, motor vehicle theft, and arson. The Violent Crime Index includes murder and nonnegligent manslaughter, forcible rape, robbery and aggravated assault.
Source: Office of Juvenile Justice and Delinquency Prevention [107]

JUVENILE DELINQUENCY: CAUSE & EFFECT

Family Background and Juvenile Delinquency

SNAPSHOT 1
Children from broken homes are more likely to engage in delinquent behavior.

- A 2000 study found that adolescents from intact families were less likely to engage in serious physical fighting, in shootings or in stabbings than were those raised by single parents, stepparents or no parents.[108]

- A 1998 study of single-parent and married-parent families concluded that children from single-parent families were more likely to lie, cheat, and destroy property, and to associate with trouble-making peers.[109]

- In 1998, a study of adolescents convicted of homicide in adult court found that at the time of the crimes, 43 percent of their parents had never been married, 30 percent were divorced and nine percent were separated.[110]

- A 2000 study of juvenile crime in rural areas revealed that broken homes were strongly associated with higher rates of juvenile arrest for violent crimes, while poverty was not directly associated with juvenile violence.[111]

- Longitudinal research on youth in three urban centers showed that the more family structure changes a child experiences, the greater his risk of delinquency.[112]

Moral poverty is the poverty of being without loving, capable, responsible adults who teach you right from wrong; the poverty of being without parents and other authorities who habituate you to feel joy at others' joy, pain at others' pain, satisfaction when you do right, remorse when you do wrong; the poverty of growing up in the virtual absence of people who teach morality by their own everyday example and who insist that you follow suit. . . . And moral poverty, not economic poverty, is what marks some disadvantaged youngsters for a life of crime while passing over others in equal or greater material distress.

—William J. Bennett,
John J. DiIulio, Jr., John P. Walters
Body Count [113]

Snapshot 2

Lack of parental involvement and adult supervision correlates with youth criminal activity.

- A study of 3,726 children age 10-14 found that those who had adult supervision after school were 23 percent less likely to skip school, use alcohol or marijuana, steal or hurt some one than were children who were unsupervised.[114]

- A 1999 study of sixth and seventh graders found that those from intact families were more likely to be home with a parent or other adult after school than were students from single-parent families, who were more likely to be with friends during after-school hours. Students who experienced little parental supervision showed more aggression, delinquency, substance abuse, and vulnerability to peer pressure.[115]

Consequences of Juvenile Delinquency

Snapshot 1

Early violent offenders frequently become chronic violent offenders.

- According to a 2003 Department of Justice report, child delinquents ages 7-12 are two to three times more likely to become serious, violent, and chronic offenders than are adolescents who first engage in delinquency in their teens.[116]

- A 1998 article on a longitudinal study in Rochester, N.Y., reported that 40 percent of children who committed violent offenses before age nine became chronic offenders by age 16. Among those who began committing violent offenses between age 10 and 12, 30 percent became chronic violent offenders, compared to 23 percent whose first violent offense was committed at age 13 or older.[117]

SNAPSHOT 2

Early juvenile delinquency can lead to social detachment and teen fatherhood.

- Longitudinal data from Rochester, N.Y., showed a reciprocal relationship between delinquency and parent-child relationships: poor parent-child relationships contributed to early delinquency, and delinquent behavior further strained parent-child relationships.[118]

- Earlier involvement in delinquency contributes to detachment from school.[119]

- Boys who engage in delinquency at an early age are likely to become teen fathers, and teen fathers are likely to engage in delinquent behavior. One study found that, compared to teens who were not fathers, teen fathers were 7.5 times more likely to engage in serious delingquency during the same year they became fathers.[120]

WHAT THE POLLS SAY ABOUT JUVENILE DELINQUENCY

Adult Attitudes

SNAPSHOT 1

Americans believe that strong marriages help deter youth violence.

- In 1998, 72 percent of Americans agreed that married parents are less likely to have children who are violent and commit crimes.

Question: "Do you agree or disagree that mothers and fathers who have strong marriages are less likely to have children or teenagers who are violent and commit crimes?"

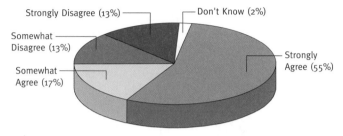

Source: Wirthlin Worldwide [121]

- When compared to other strategies, Americans think that the best solution to youth violence is for married parents to stay together and to stay involved in their children's lives.

Question: "Which of the following do you believe would be the best solution to the problem of youth violence: parents who commit to maintaining a strong marriage and stay involved in their kids' lives, teaching moral principles to youth, positive role models who participate in kids' lives or less violence on TV, in movies, and in music?"

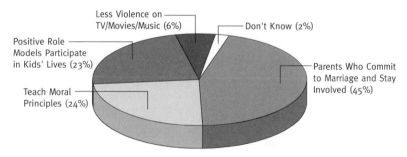

Source: Wirthlin Worldwide [122]

SNAPSHOT 2
Lack of parental supervision and poor parent-child relationships are seen as major contributors to youth violence.

• In a 2001 poll, 86 percent said a lack of adult supervision of children contributes greatly to violence in society.

Question: "Our society is often described as being more inclined toward violence than some others. Do you think that ... lack of adult supervision of children ... contributes a lot, contributes a little, or doesn't contribute at all to this violence?"

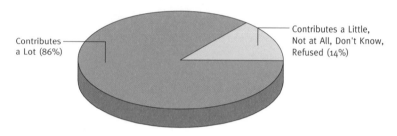

Contributes a Lot (86%)

Contributes a Little, Not at All, Don't Know, Refused (14%)

Source: Harris Poll [123]

• Nearly all respondents in a 2001 poll said students' home lives and relationships with their parents were very important factors leading to the school shootings of recent years.

Question: "How important do you think [the home life students have today, including their relationship with their parents] is as a cause of the school shootings that have been occurring?"

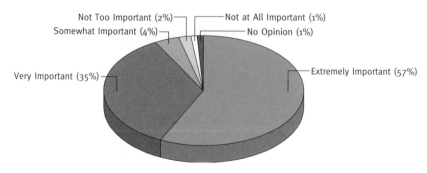

Not Too Important (2%)
Somewhat Important (4%)
Not at All Important (1%)
No Opinion (1%)
Very Important (35%)
Extremely Important (57%)

Source: Gallup Poll [124]

- In a 2000 poll, nearly all respondents said a lack of moral training in the home is a critical or important cause of crime.

Question: "While some people view all of these as important causes of crime, we'd like to know which factors you think are the most important. As I read each item, please tell me whether you think it is a critical factor, a very important factor, a somewhat important factor or not an important factor. How about a lack of moral training in the home?"

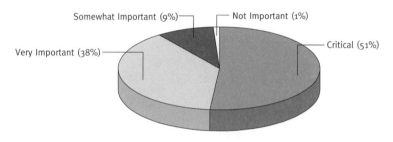

Somewhat Important (9%) Not Important (1%)

Very Important (38%) Critical (51%)

Source: Gallup Poll [125]

Teen Attitudes

SNAPSHOT 1
Nearly all teens believe youth violence is a problem today.

- In a 1998 survey, nine out of 10 teens said they believed youth violence is a problem today.

Question: "To what degree do you feel youth violence is a problem in our country today?"

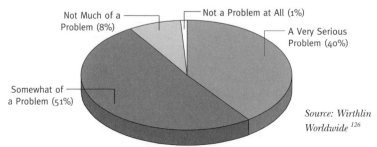

Not Much of a Problem (8%) Not a Problem at All (1%)

A Very Serious Problem (40%)

Somewhat of a Problem (51%)

Source: Wirthlin Worldwide [126]

SNAPSHOT 2
Most teens see a father's absence as a factor in youth violence.

- In 1998, 67 percent of youth surveyed thought that father absence was linked to juvenile delinquency.

Question: "Do you feel youth are more likely to be violent and commit crimes when their fathers are absent from the home?"

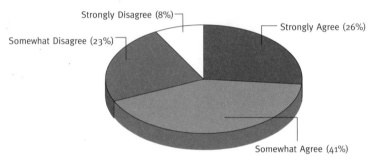

Strongly Disagree (8%)
Somewhat Disagree (23%)
Strongly Agree (26%)
Somewhat Agree (41%)

Source: Wirthlin Worldwide [127]

SNAPSHOT 3
Teens see drug use as a key cause of youth violence.

- A 1998 survey found that 31 percent of teens polled cited youth drug abuse as the leading cause of youth violence.

Question: "Which of the following do you believe is the leading cause of youth violence in our country today?"

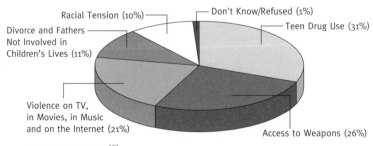

Racial Tension (10%)
Divorce and Fathers Not Involved in Children's Lives (11%)
Violence on TV, in Movies, in Music and on the Internet (21%)
Don't Know/Refused (1%)
Teen Drug Use (31%)
Access to Weapons (26%)

Source: Wirthlin Worldwide [128]

CHAPTER 16

Suicide among Youth

For young people 15-24 years old, suicide is the third leading cause of death, behind unintentional injury and homicide. In 1999, more teenagers and young adults died from suicide than from cancer, heart disease, AIDS, birth defects, stroke, pneumonia and influenza and chronic lung disease **combined**.

—Centers for Disease Control
Suicide in the United States

BY THE NUMBERS: SUICIDE AMONG YOUTH

SNAPSHOT 1

While the suicide rate among young adults age 20-24 decreased between 1980 and 2000, the rate among young adolescents nearly doubled.

- Between 1980 and 2000, the suicide rate among 10- to 14-year-olds nearly doubled.

Suicide Rates among Youth, 1980-2000

Note: Suicide rate is the annual number of suicides per 100,000 youth.
Source: Centers for Disease Control [129]

SNAPSHOT 2

The number of suicides among older adolescents peaked in 1988 and then declined during the 1990s.

- The number of suicides among 15- to 19-year-olds peaked in 1988 at 2,059 and then declined to 1,621 in 2000.

Number of Suicides among 15- to 19-Year-Olds

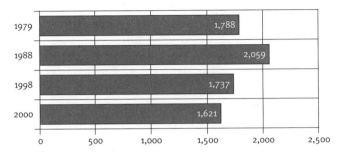

1979	1,788
1988	2,059
1998	1,737
2000	1,621

0   500   1,000   1,500   2,000   2,500

Number of Suicides among Youth, 1979-2000

Year	Age 10-14	Age 15-19	Age 20-24
1979	151	1,788	3,458
1980	139	1,797	3,442
1982	198	1,730	3,295
1984	225	1,692	3,334
1986	250	1,896	3,224
1988	237	2,059	2,870
1990	258	1,979	2,890
1992	304	1,847	2,846
1994	318	1,948	3,008
1996	298	1,817	2,541
1998	317	1,737	2,398
2000	300	1,621	2,373

Source: Centers for Disease Control[130]

Snapshot 3
Suicide is a leading cause of death among youth.

- After unintentional injury and homicide, suicide is the third leading cause of death among 15- to 24-year-olds. Among all Americans, suicide is the 11th leading cause of death.[131]

- In 2000, 15 percent of all suicides occurred among people under age 25.[132]

- Between 1952 and 1995, the incidence of suicide among adolescents and young adults nearly tripled.[133]

SNAPSHOT 4
Males are more likely than females to commit suicide.

- In 1998, 80 percent of all suicides were committed by males. Boys age 15-19 were five times more likely to commit suicide than were girls. Among 20- to 24-year-olds, males were seven times more likely to commit suicide.[134]

- Females attempt suicide more often than do males, but males are four times more likely to die from suicide.[135]

- From 1980-1996, the suicide rate among black males age 15-19 increased 105 percent.[136]

FAMILY BACKGROUND AND YOUTH SUICIDE

SNAPSHOT 1
Children in intact families are less likely to commit suicide.

- According to a Swedish study of almost a million children, children raised by single parents are more than twice as likely as those raised in two-parent homes to suffer from a serious psychiatric disorder, to commit or attempt suicide or to develop an alcohol addiction.[137]

- A 2000 Norwegian study found that adolescents living with either a single parent or neither biological parent were twice as likely to attempt suicide than were those living with both parents.[138]

- A 1998 study found that adolescents from broken homes were more likely to be suicidal than were adolescents from intact families. Thirty-eight percent of teens in stepfamilies were suicidal, compared to 20 percent in single-parent homes and only nine percent in intact families. Adolescents from emotionally close families who spent time together were less likely to be suicidal.[139]

- Teens' connectedness to parents, including shared activities and high parental expectations, protects against serious emotional distress and suicide, according to the 1997 Adolescent Health study of 12,000 youth.[140]

WHAT THE POLLS SAY ABOUT YOUTH SUICIDE

Adult Responses

SNAPSHOT 1
Americans do not consider themselves knowledgeable about the symptoms of suicidal teenagers.

Question: "How much do you know about the symptoms or signs that may indicate that a teenager is considering suicide—a great deal, some, a little, hardly anything, or nothing at all?"

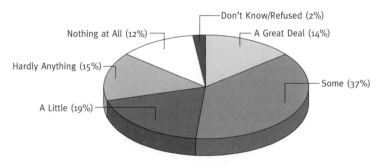

Don't Know/Refused (2%)
Nothing at All (12%)
A Great Deal (14%)
Hardly Anything (15%)
Some (37%)
A Little (19%)

Source: Time, CNN [141]

SNAPSHOT 2

Many Americans do not think suicide is a major issue for teens.

Question: "I am going to read you a list of issues that teens may face. For each one, please tell me how big a problem you think it is for teens in general—a major problem, a minor problem, or not a problem at all . . . Suicide."

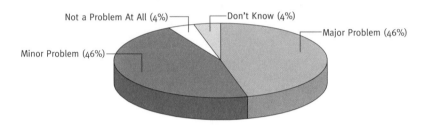

Source: Princeton Survey Research [142]

Teen Responses

SNAPSHOT 1

Almost half of teens know peers who have attempted suicide.

- In 2004, 45 percent of teens age 13-17 said they knew someone their age who has attempted suicide.

Question: "Do you personally know of any teenagers who have tried to commit suicide?"

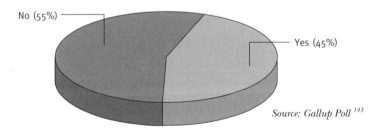

Source: Gallup Poll [143]

N O T E S

CHAPTER 11 Teen Sex

1   Centers for Disease Control, "Trends in Sexual Risk Behaviors Among High School
     Students – United States, 1991-2001," *Morbidity and Mortality Weekly Report,* Volume
     51, September 27, 2002 and "Youth Risk Behavior Surveillance – United States,
     2003," *Morbidity and Mortality Weekly Report,* Volume 53, May 21, 2004.

2   Ibid.

3   Joyce C. Abma and Freya L. Sonenstein, *Sexual Activity and Contraceptive Practices
     Among Teenagers in the United States, 1988 and 1995,* Series 23: Data from the National
     Survey of Family Growth, National Center for Health Statistics, April 2001, Table 1.

4   Centers for Disease Control, "Youth Risk Behavior Surveillance – United States,
     2003."

5   John. S. Santelli, et al., "The Association of Sexual Behaviors with Socioeconomic
     Status, Family Structure, and Race/Ethnicity Among U.S. Adolescents," *American
     Journal of Public Health* 90 (October 2000): 1582-1588.

6   Rosalie J. Bakken and Mary Winter, "Family Characteristics and Sexual Risk
     Behaviors Among Black Men in the United States," *Perspectives on Sexual and
     Reproductive Health* 34 (September/October 2002): 252-258.

7   Dawn Upchurch, et al., "Gender and Ethnic Differences in the Timing of First
     Sexual Intercourse," *Family Planning Perspectives* 30 (May/June 1998): 121-127.

8   Kathleen Mullan Harris, et al., "Evaluating the Role of 'Nothing to Lose' Attitudes
     on Risky Behavior in Adolescence," *Social Forces* 80 (March 2002): 1005-1037.

9   Michael D. Resnick, et al., "Protecting Adolescents from Harm: Findings from the
     National Longitudinal Study on Adolescent Health," *Journal of American Medicine* 278
     (September 10, 1997): 823-832.

10   Christina Olenik Lynch, "Risk and Protective Factors Associated with Adolescent
     Sexual Activity," *Adolescent & Family Health* 2 (2001): 99-107.

11   Deborah A. Cohen, et al., "When and Where Do Youths Have Sex? The Potential
     Role of Adult Supervision," *Pediatrics* 110 (December 2002): 1-6.

12   The Alan Guttmacher Institute, "Teen Sex and Pregnancy," *Facts in Brief,* 1999.

13   Linda L. Alexander, ed., et al., "Sexually Transmitted Diseases in America: How Many
     Cases and at What Cost?" The Kaiser Family Foundation, December 1998, p. 8.

14   Hillard Weinstock, et al., "Sexually Transmitted Diseases Among American Youth:
     Incidence and Prevalence Estimates, 2000."

15   Centers for Disease Control, *Tracking the Hidden Epidemics: Trends in STDs in the
     United States: 2000,* p. 4.

16   The Kaiser Family Foundation, "Sexually Transmitted Diseases in the U.S.," June
     2003.

17   The Medical Institute for Sexual Health, "Medical Updates: Frequently Asked
     Questions," Available at *www.medinstitute.org/medical/faq.htm* and The Alan
     Guttmacher Institute, "Teen Sex and Pregnancy."

18   Harrell W. Chesson, et al., "The Estimated Direct Medical Cost of Sexually Transmitted Diseases Among American Youth, 2000," *Perspectives on Sexual and Reproductive Health* 36 (January/February 2004): 11-19.

19   William L. Yarber, "Selected Risk and Protective Factors Associated With Two or More Lifetime Sexual Intercourse Partners and Non-Condom Use During Last Coitus Among U.S. Rural High School Students," *American Journal of Health Education* 33 (July, August 2002): 206-213.

20   Lydia O'Donnell and Carl O'Donnell, "Early Sexual Initiation and Subsequent Sex-Related Risks Among Urban Minority Youth: The Reach for Health Study," *Family Planning Perspectives* 33 (November/December 2001): 268-275, as cited by The Medical Institute for Sexual Health, "The Medical Institute Advisory," February 5, 2002.

21   Rosalie J. Bakken and Mary Winter, "Family Characteristics and Sexual Risk Behaviors Among Black Men in the United States."

22   Tom and Judy Lickona, *Sex, Love And You* (Notre Dame: Ave Maria Press, 1994), pp. 62-77.

23   Robert E. Rector, et al., "Sexually Active Teenagers Are More Likely To Be Depressed and to Attempt Suicide," A Report of The Heritage Center for Data Analysis, The Heritage Foundation, June 3, 2003.

24   General Social Survey, National Opinion Research Center, February 6 – June 26, 2002.

25   Princeton Survey Research Associates for Newsweek, April 20-28, 2000.

26   The Polling Company for Family Research Council, November 3-4, 1998, as cited in "The Common Sense: Voters' Opinion on Key Issues," Family Research Council, Washington, DC, 1998, pp. 23-24.

27   Zogby International for Focus on the Family, "Survey on Parental Opinions of Character- or Relationship-Based Abstinence Education vs. Comprehensive Sex Education," January 2004.

28   Ibid.

29   International Communications Research for National Campaign to Prevent Teen Pregnancy, as cited in "With One Voice 2003: America's Adults and Teens Sound Off About Teen Pregnancy," National Campaign to Prevent Teen Pregnancy, December 2003.

30   International Communications Research for National Campaign to Prevent Teen Pregnancy, as cited in "The Cautious Generation? Teens Tell Us about Sex, Virginity and 'The Talk'," National Campaign to Prevent Teen Pregnancy, April 27, 2000.

31   International Communications Research for National Campaign to Prevent Teen Pregnancy, as cited in "With One Voice 2003: America's Adults and Teens Sound Off About Teen Pregnancy."

32   Ibid.

33   The Kaiser Family Foundation and *Seventeen Magazine*, "Virginity and The First Time," October 2003.

34   Scott Boggess and Carolyn Bradner, "Trends in Adolescent Males' Abortion Attitudes, 1988-1995: Differences by Race and Ethnicity," *Family Planning Perspectives* 32 (May/June 2000): 118-123.

35   American Freshman Survey, UCLA's Higher Education Research Institute, 1990 and 2001.

36   International Communications Research for National Campaign to Prevent Teen Pregnancy, as cited in "With One Voice 2003: America's Adults and Teens Sound Off About Teen Pregnancy."

CHAPTER 12 Teen Unwed Childbearing

37   Stephanie Ventura, et al., *Nonmarital Childbearing in the United States, 1940-99*, National Vital Statistics Reports 48, National Center for Health Statistics, October 18, 2000, Table 4 and Joyce A. Martin, et al., *Births Final Data for 2002*, National Vital Statistics Reports 52, National Center for Health Statistics, December 17, 2003, Table 17.

38   Stephanie Ventura, et al., *Nonmarital Childbearing in the United States, 1940-99*, Table 3 and Joyce A. Martin, *Births: Final Data for 2002*, Table 18.

39   Joyce A. Martin, et al., *Births: Final Data for 2002*, Table 18.

40   Joanna K. Mohn, et al., "An Analysis of the Causes of the Decline in Non-marital Birth and Pregnancy Rates for Teens from 1991 to 1995," *Adolescent & Family Health* 3 (2003): 39-47.

41   Joyce A. Martin, et al., *Births: Final Data for 2002*, Table B.

42   Sara McLanahan and Gary Sandefur, *Growing Up with a Single Parent: What Hurts, What Helps* (Cambridge: Harvard University Press, 1994), pp. 1-2.

43   Kristin A Moore, et al., "Nonmarital School-Age Motherhood: Family Individual, and School Characteristics," *Journal of Adolescent Research* 13 (October 1998): 433-457.

44   Bruce J. Ellis and John E. Bates, et al., "Does Father Absence Place Daughters at Special Risk for Early Sexual Activity and Teenage Pregnancy?" *Child Development* 74 (May/June 2003): 801-821.

45   Jennifer Manlove, "Subsequent Fertility Among Teen Mothers: Longitudinal Analyses of Recent National Data," *Journal of Marriage and the Family* 62 (May 2000): 430-448.

46   Patricia J. Dittus and James Jaccard, "Adolescents' Perceptions of Maternal Disapproval of Sex: Relationship to Sexual Outcomes," *Journal of Adolescent Health* 26 (2000): 268-278.

47   Christine M. Markham, et al., "Family Connectedness and Sexual Risk-Taking Among Urban Youth Attending Alternative High Schools," *Perspectives on Sexual and Reproductive Health* 35 (July/August 2003): 174-179.

48   Rebecca A. Maynard, *Kids Having Kids: Economic and Social Consequences of Teen Pregnancy* (Washington, D.C.: Urban Institute Press, 1997), pp. 2-5.

49   Ibid.

50   Ibid.

51   Ibid.

52   Ariel Kalil and James Kunz, "Teenage Childbearing, Marital Status, and Depressive Symptoms in Later Life," *Child Development* 73 (December 2002): 1748-1760.

53   Judith Levine and Harold Pollack, et al., "Academic and Behavioral Outcomes Among the Children of Young Mothers," *Journal of Marriage and Family* 63 (May 2001): 355-369.

54   Amy Conseur, et al., "Maternal and Perinatal Risk Factors for Later Delinquency," *Pediatrics* 99 (June 1997): 785-790.

55   Rebecca A. Maynard, pp. 205-229, 257-281.

56   Sandra L. Hofferth and Lori Reid, "Early Childbearing and Children's Achievement and Behavior over Time," *Perspectives on Sexual and Reproductive Health* 34 (January/February 2002): 41-49.

57   Rebecca Maynard, ed., *Kids Having Kids: A Robin Hood Foundation Special Report on the Costs of Adolescent Childbearing*, The Robin Hood Foundation, New York, 1996, p. 19.

58   Ibid, p. 20.

59   Princeton Survey Research Associates for NPR, Kaiser Family Foundation, and Harvard University Kennedy School of Government, "Sex Education in America Survey," September 29 – October 23, 2003.

60   Princeton Survey Research Associates for the Kaiser Family Foundation, July 7- September 19, 1999, Available at *www.publicagenda.org/issues/pcc_detail2.cfm ?issue_type=family&concern_graphic=pcc8.gif.*

61   Monitoring the Future Study conducted by the Survey Research Center, University of Michigan as cited in The National Marriage Project, *The State of Our Unions 2003: The Social Health of Marriage in America*, June 2003, p. 32.

62   International Communications Research for National Campaign to Prevent Teen Pregnancy, as cited in "With One Voice 2003: America's Adults and Teens Sound Off About Teen Pregnancy."

CHAPTER 13   Teen Abortion

63   Stanley K. Henshaw, "U.S. Teenage Pregnancy Statistics With Comparative Statistics for Women Aged 20-24," Alan Guttmacher Institute, May 1, 2003.

64   Ibid.

65   Alan Guttmacher Institute, "Abortion in the U.S.," January 2003.

66   The Alan Guttmacher Institute, "U.S. Teenage Pregnancy Statistics: Overall Trends, Trends by Race and Ethnicity and State-by-State Information," February 19, 2004.

67   American Freshman Survey, UCLA's Higher Education Research Institute, 1987-2003.

68   Gallup Organization, "Teens Lean Conservative on Abortion," November 18, 2003.

69   Scott Boggess and Carolyn Bradner, "Trends in Adolescent Males' Abortion Attitudes, 1988-1995."

CHAPTER 14   Teen Drug and Alcohol Abuse

70   Illicit drugs include marijuana, LSD, other hallucinogens, crack, other cocaine, heroin, or any use of narcotics, amphetamines, barbiturates or tranquilizers not pre-scribed by a doctor. Lloyd D. Johnston, et al., "Monitoring the Future National Results on Adolescent Drug Use: Overview of Key Findings: 2002," National Institute on Drug Abuse, Bethesda, Maryland, 2003.

71   Ibid.

72   Ibid.

73 Ibid.

74 Ibid.

75 Ibid.

76 Ibid.

77 Terrence P. Thornberry, et al., "Family Disruption and Delinquency," *Juvenile Justice Bulletin*, Office of Juvenile Justice and Delinquency Prevention, U.S. Department of Justice, September 1999, p. 4, Available at *www.ncjrs.org/html/ojjdp/9909-1/contents.html.*

78 Jerome L. Short, "Predictors of Substance Use and Mental Health of Children of Divorce: A Prospective Analysis," *Journal of Divorce and Remarriage* 29 (1998): 147-166.

79 Shanta R. Dube, et al., "Childhood Abuse, Neglect and Household Dysfunction and the Risk of Illicit Drug Use: The Adverse Childhood Experiences Study," *Pediatrics* 111 (March 2003): 564-572.

80 Gunilla Ringback Weitoft, et al., "Mortality, Severe Morbidity and Injury in Children Living with Single Parents in Sweden: A Population-based Study," *The Lancet* 361 (January 25, 2003): 289-295.

81 Deborah A. Cohen, et al., "When and Where Do Youths Have Sex? The Potential Role of Adult Supervision," *Pediatrics* 110 (December 2002): 1-6.

82 Laura De Haan and Rikki Trageton, "Relationships between Substance Use Information and Use Prevalence and Attitudes," *Adolescent & Family Health* 2 (Summer 2001): 55-61.

83 National Center on Addiction and Substance Abuse at Columbia University, "The Importance of Family Dinners," September 2003.

84 The National Clearinghouse for Alcohol and Drug Information, "Consequences of Underage Alcohol Use," SAMHSA Fact Sheet, U.S. Department of Health and Human Services, Available at *www.health.org/govpubs/rpo992/.*

85 The National Center on Addiction and Substance Abuse, "Non-Medical Marijuana: Rite of Passage or Russian Roulette?" CASA White Paper, Columbia University, July 1999, p. 3.

86 Michael T. Lynskey, et al., "Escalation of Drug Use in Early-Onset Cannabis Users vs. Co-twin Controls," *Journal of the American Medical Association* 289 (January 22-29, 2003): 427-433.

87 Ralph Hingson, et al., "Early Age of First Drunkenness as a Factor in College Students' Unplanned and Unprotected Sex Attributable to Drinking," *Pediatrics* 111 (January 2003): 34-41.

88 The National Clearinghouse for Alcohol and Drug Information, "Consequences of Underage Alcohol Use," Available at *www.health.org/govpubs/rpo992/.*

89 Ibid.

90 National Institute on Drug Abuse, "Info Facts: Marijuana," Available at *www.nida.hih.gov/Infofax/marijuana.html.*

91 The Kaiser Family Foundation, "Substance Use and Risky Sexual Behavior: Attitudes and Practices Among Adolescents and Young Adults," February 2002.

92 The National Center on Addiction and Substance Abuse, "Dangerous Liaisons: Substance Abuse and Sex," CASA White Paper, Columbia University, July 1999, p. 36.

93   The National Clearinghouse for Alcohol and Drug Information, "Teen Marijuana Users Report Psychosocial Problems," SAMHSA News, Summer, 1998, pp. 2-4.

94   Office of National Drug Control Policy, "Juveniles and Drugs," Fact Sheet, NCJ 196879, June 2003.

95   Princeton Survey Research Associates for NPR, Kaiser Family Foundation and Harvard University Kennedy School of Government, September 29 – October 23, 2003.

96   Princeton Survey Research Associates for Pew Research Center, February 14-19, 2001.

97   National Center on Addiction and Substance Abuse, "Teen Tipplers: America's Underage Drinking Epidemic," February 2003.

98   Lloyd D. Johnston, et al., "Monitoring the Future National Results on Adolescent Drug Use: Overview of Key Findings: 2002."

99   Ibid.

100   Ibid.

CHAPTER 15   Juvenile Delinquency

101   David Blankenhorn, *Fatherless America* (New York: BasicBooks, 1995), p. 31.

102   Bureau of Justice Statistics, *Sourcebook of Criminal Justice Statistics 1993*, Table 4.18, U.S. Department of Justice, 1994, page 403.

103   Office of Juvenile Justice and Delinquency Prevention, "Juvenile Arrest Rates for Violent Crime Index Offenses, 1980-2001, " OJJDP Statistical Briefing Book, Available at *http://ojjdp.ncjrs.org/ojstatbb/asp/JAR_Display.asp?ID=qa0520120030531* and "Juvenile Arrest Rates for All Crimes, 1980-2001," Available at *http://ojjdp.ncjrs.org/ojstatbb/asp/JAR_Display.asp?ID=qa0520020030531.*

104   Howard Snyder, "Juvenile Arrests 2001," Juvenile Justice Bulletin, Office of Juvenile Justice and Delinquency Prevention, U.S. Department of Justice, December 2003.

105   Howard Snyder, "Juvenile Arrests 2001."

106   Ibid.

107   Office of Juvenile Justice and Delinquency Prevention, "Juvenile Arrest Rates for Property Crime Index Offenses by Sex, 1980-2001," Statistical Briefing Book, Available at *http://ojjdp.ncjrs.org/ojstatbb/asp/JAR_Display.asp?ID=qa0523620030531* and "Juvenile Arrest Rates for Violent Crime Index Offenses by Sex, 1980-2001," Available at *http://ojjdp.ncjrs.org/ojstatbb/asp/JAR_Display.asp?ID=qa0523120030531.*

108   Todd M. Franke, "The Role of Attachment as a Protective Factor in Adolescent Violent Behavior," *Adolescent & Family Health* 1 (Winter 2000): 40-57.

109   Jeanne M. Hilton and Esther L. Devall, "Comparison of Parenting and Children's Behavior in Single-Mother, Single-Father, and Intact Families," *Journal of Divorce and Remarriage* 29 (1998): 23-54.

110   Patrick J. Darby, et al., "Analysis of 112 Juveniles Who Committed Homicide: Characteristics and a Closer Look at Family Abuse," *Journal of Family Violence* 13 (1998): 365-374.

111   D. Wayne Osgood and Jeff M. Chambers, "Social Disorganization Outside the Metropolis: An Analysis of Rural Youth Violence," *Criminology* 38 (2000): 81-115.

112 Terrence P. Thornberry, et al., "Family Disruption and Delinquency."

113 William J. Bennett, John DiIulio, Jr., et al., *Body Count: Moral Poverty ... and How to Win America's War Against Crime and Drugs* (New York: Simon & Schuster, 1996), p. 56.

114 Anna Aizer, "Home Alone: Supervision After School and Child Behavior, *Journal of Public Economics*, forthcoming.

115 Daniel J. Flannery, et al., "Who Are They With and What Are They Doing? Delinquent Behavior, Substance Use, and Early Adolescents' After-School Time," *American Journal of Orthopsychiatry* 69 (April 1999): 247-253.

116 Howard N. Snyder, et al., "Prevalence and Development of Child Delinquency," *Child Delinquency Bulletin Series*, Office of Juvenile Justice and Delinquency Prevention, March 2003.

117 Linda L. Dahlberg, "Youth Violence in the United States: Major Trends, Risk Factors, and Prevention Approaches," *American Journal of Preventive Medicine* 14 (1998): 261-262.

118 Katharine Browning, et al., "Highlights of Findings from the Rochester Youth Development Study," OJJDP Fact Sheet 103, Office of Juvenile Justice and Delinquency Prevention, U.S. Department of Justice, April 1999.

119 Ibid., and Linda L. Dahlberg, "Youth Violence in the United States," p. 262.

120 Terence P. Thornberry, et al., "Teenage Fatherhood and Delinquent Behavior," Juvenile Justice Bulletin, Office of Juvenile Justice and Delinquency Prevention, January 2000.

121 Wirthlin Worldwide for Family First, September 11-17, 1998, as cited in H. Chris Slane, *Kids & Violence: A National Survey and Report*, Family First, Tampa, Florida, p. 21.

122 Ibid., p.23.

123 Harris Poll, March 22 - 26, 2001.

124 Gallup Poll, March 26-28, 2001.

125 Gallup Poll, March 20, 2001, as cited in Bureau of Justice Statistics, *The Sourcebook of Criminal Justice Statistics*, 2001, p.128.

126 Wirthlin Worldwide for Family First, September 11-17, 1998, as cited in H. Chris Slane, *Kids & Violence: A National Survey and Report*, p. 9.

127 Ibid., p. 18.

128 Ibid., p. 12.

CHAPTER 16 Suicide Among Youth

129 Centers for Disease Control, "Death Rates for 72 Selected Causes by 5-Year Age Groups, Race, and Sex: United States, 1979-98," Table 291, Available at *www.cdc.gov/nchs/datawh/statab/unpubd/mortabs/gmwk291.htm* and Centers for Disease Control and Prevention., Web-based Injury Statistics Query and Reporting System (WISQARS), Available at *http://www.cdc.gov/ncipc/wisqars*.

130 Centers for Disease Control, "Death Rates for 72 Selected Causes by 5-Year Age Groups, Race and Sex: United States, 1979-98," Table 291A and Web-based Injury Statistics Query and Reporting System (WISQARS).

131 Centers for Disease Control, "Suicide in the United States," Available at *www.cdc.gov/ncipc/factsheets/suifacts.htm.*

132 Ibid.

133 Ibid.

134 Centers for Disease Control, "Injury Fact Book, 2001-2002," Available at *http://www.cdc.gov/ncipc/fact_book/26_Suicide.htm.*

135 Ibid.

136 Centers for Disease Control, "Suicide in the United States."

137 Gunilla Ringback Weitoft, et al., "Mortality, Severe Morbidity and Injury in Children Living with Single Parents in Sweden: A Population-based Study."

138 Lars Wichstrom, "Predictors of Adolescent Suicide Attempts: A Nationally Representative Longitudinal Study of Norwegian Adolescents," *Journal of the American Academy of Child Adolescent Psychiatry* 39 (2000): 603-610.

139 Judith Rubenstein, et al., "Suicidal Behavior in Adolescents: Stress and Protection in Different Family Contexts," *American Journal of Orthopsychiatry* 68 (1998): 274-284.

140 Michael D. Resnick, et al., "Protecting Adolescents from Harm: Findings from the National Longitudinal Study on Adolescent Health."

141 Harris Interactive for *Time,* CNN, September 26-28, 2001.

142 Princeton Survey Research Associates for NPR, Kaiser Family Foundation and Harvard University Kennedy School of Government, September 29 – October 23, 2003.

143 Collen McMurray, "Nearly Half of Teens Aware of Peer Suicide Attempts," The Gallup Organization, May 25, 2004.

CHAPTER 17

Family Formation around the World

In some parts of Europe . . . fertility has fallen to an average of .85 children born to women over their lifetime, barely 40 percent of even the zero-growth level. In northern Europe, marriage has been replaced by low-fertility cohabitating unions. In southern Europe, young men and women refuse to form unions of any kind. Fertility decline has been particularly striking since 1990. By 2050, in consequence, most young Europeans will have neither brother or sister, nor aunt nor uncle, nor cousins: so undoing even the extended family.

—Dr. Allan C. Carlson
"The Fertility Gap: Recrafting American
Population Policy for a Depopulating World"
Family Policy Lecture, Family Research Council
April 24, 2003

Snapshot 1
Around the world, men and women are marrying at later ages.

- In Sweden, the mean age of women at first marriage was 30 in 2000, compared to 24 in 1970.

- In Germany, the mean age of women at first marriage was 27 in 1999, compared to 23 in 1970.

Mean Age of Women at First Marriage

		EARLIER DATE		LATER DATE	
COUNTRY	YEAR	MEAN AGE OF WOMEN AT FIRST MARRIAGE	YEAR	MEAN AGE OF WOMEN AT FIRST MARRIAGE
Austria	1970	22.9	2000	27.2
Belgium	1970	22.4	1999	26.1
Czech Republic	1970	21.6	2000	24.9
Denmark	1970	22.8	2000	29.5
Finland	1970	23.3	2000	28.0
France	1970	22.6	2000	27.8
Germany	1970	22.5	1999	27.2
Greece	1970	24.0	1999	26.6
Hungary	1970	21.5	2000	24.6
Iceland	1970	23.2	2000	29.9
Ireland	1970	24.8	1996	28.2
Italy	1970	23.9	1997	27.0
Japan	1970	24.2	2000	27.0
Netherlands	1970	22.9	2000	27.8
Norway	1970	22.8	1999	28.6
Poland	1970	22.8	1998	23.6
Portugal	1970	24.0	2000	25.2
Romania	1970	21.8	2000	23.4
Russia	1970	23.2	1996	22.1
Slovakia	1970	22.0	2000	24.0
Spain	1970	24.8	1999	27.7
Sweden	1970	23.9	2000	30.2
Switzerland	1970	24.2	2000	27.9
United Kingdom	1970	22.4	1999	27.3
United States	**1970**	**21.8**	**1998**	**26.4**

Source: United Nations [1]

Snapshot 2
Nearly all nations have experienced a decline in the total first marriage rate since the 1970s.

- The total first marriage rate for France indicated that in 1970, 92 percent of French women would have married at least once by age 50, compared to only 62 percent in 2000.

Total First Marriage Rates among Women

	EARLIER DATE		LATER DATE	
COUNTRY	YEAR	TOTAL FIRST MARRIAGE RATE	YEAR	TOTAL FIRST MARRIAGE RATE
Australia	1976	.78	1996	.60
Austria	1970	.91	2000	.54
Belgium	1980	.77	2000	.52
Canada	1975	.81	1997	.66
Czech Republic	1970	.91	2000	.50
Denmark	1970	.82	2000	.73
Finland	1970	.94	2000	.62
France	1970	.92	2000	.62
Germany	1970	.98	2000	.58
Greece	1970	1.06	2000	.52
Hungary	1970	.97	2000	.49
Iceland	1975	.79	1999	.62
Italy	1970	1.01	1999	.62
Japan	1975	.82	1998	.70
Netherlands	1970	1.06	2000	.59
New Zealand	1975	.81	1998	.52
Norway	1970	.96	1999	.52
Poland	1970	.91	2000	.63
Portugal	1970	1.21	2000	.73
Republic of Korea	N/A	N/A	1998	.66
Romania	1970	.84	2000	.64
Russia	1970	1.06	1996	.60
Sweden	1970	.62	2000	.53
Switzerland	1970	.87	2000	.64
Ukraine	1970	1.04	1995	.53
United Kingdom	1970	1.04	1999	.53
United States	**1975**	**.62**	**1990**	**.59**

Source: United Nations [2]

Total first marriage rate is the proportion of women who would have ever married at least once by age 50, if the age-specific first marriage rates observed in a given year applied throughout life. A figure at or near 1.0 reflects a culture where marriage is nearly universal among adult women.

SNAPSHOT 3
Over the past four decades, the total divorce rate has increased among nearly all nations.

- In 1999, the total divorce rate in Norway was three times higher than it was in 1970.

- Between 1970 and 1999, the total divorce rate in Belgium increased four-fold.

Total Divorce Rates among Women

COUNTRY	EARLIER DATE		LATER DATE	
	YEAR	TOTAL DIVORCE RATE	YEAR	TOTAL DIVORCE RATE
Australia	1970	.13	1996	.33
Austria	1970	.18	2000	.43
Belgium	1970	.10	1999	.44
Canada	1973	.21	1995	.29
Czech Republic	1970	.26	2000	.43
Denmark	1970	.25	2000	.45
Finland	1970	.17	2000	.51
France	1970	.12	1998	.38
Germany	1970	.17	1999	.39
Greece	1970	.05	1999	.16
Hungary	1970	.25	2000	.38
Iceland	1970	.18	2000	.39
Italy	1970	.05	1997	.10
Japan	1970	.06	1997	.16
Netherlands	1970	.11	2000	.38
New Zealand	1970	.13	1997	.30
Norway	1970	.13	1999	.40
Portugal	1970	.01	2000	.26
Republic of Korea	1979	.05	1997	.18
Romania	1970	.05	2000	.19
Russia	1970	.34	1998	.51
Sweden	1970	.23	2000	.55
Switzerland	1970	.15	2000	.26
Ukraine	1970	.29	1995	.40
United Kingdom	1970	.16	1998	.43
United States	1970	.23	1990	.25

Source: United Nations [3]

Total divorce rate is defined as the number of divorces women would have gone through by age 50, if the age-specific divorce rates observed in a given year applied throughout life.

SNAPSHOT 4
Cohabitation is very common in western and northern Europe.

- Among Swedish women born between 1960 and 1965 who had entered their first partnership by age 25, 74 percent were in a cohabiting relationship and only 6 percent married without having first cohabited.

- Among Austrian women born between 1960 and 1965 who had entered their first partnership by age 25, 55 percent were in a cohabiting relationship, while only 22 percent married without having first cohabited.

Percent of Women Marrying or Cohabiting by Age 25*

| COUNTRY | TYPE OF FIRST PARTNERSHIP | |
	MARRIAGE (NOT PRECEDED BY COHABITATION)	COHABITATION
Austria	21.7	54.6
Belgium	58.8	16.9
Canada	31.9	42.3
France	32.9	46.0
Hungary	65.7	18.1
Italy	49.8	5.0
Latvia	54.0	28.6
Lithuania	68.8	10.5
Netherlands	31.3	45.2
Norway	21.0	57.6
Poland	69.9	4.1
Portugal	55.1	10.8
Slovenia	43.5	36.0
Spain	53.2	7.3
Sweden	5.7	74.1
Switzerland	15.2	50.9

Includes only women born between 1960 and 1965.

Source: United Nations [4]

Snapshot 5

Among virtually all developed nations, the total fertility rate is
below the replacement level of 2.1 births per woman throughout
her lifetime.

- Among western European nations, Italy and Spain have the
  lowest total fertility rates.

- Between 1960 and 2000, the total fertility rates in Australia
  and New Zealand declined by about 50 percent.

Total Fertility Rates

Country	Earlier Date Year	Earlier Date Total Fertility Rate	Later Date Year	Later Date Total Fertility Rate
Australia	1960	3.45	2000	1.75
Austria	1960	2.70	2001	1.31
Belgium	1960	2.54	2000	1.66
Bulgaria	1960	2.32	2001	1.24
Canada	1960	3.81	1997	1.55
Czech Republic	1960	2.09	2001	1.14
Denmark	1960	2.54	2001	1.74
Finland	1960	2.71	2001	1.73
France	1960	2.73	2000	1.89
Germany	1960	2.37	2000	1.38
Greece	1960	2.23	1999	1.28
Iceland	1960	3.88	2000	2.08
Ireland	1960	3.76	2001	1.98
Italy	1960	2.41	2000	1.24
Japan	1960	2.02	2000	1.35
Netherlands	1960	3.12	2001	1.71
New Zealand	1960	4.11	2000	2.01
Norway	1960	2.91	2001	1.78
Poland	1969	2.98	2001	1.29
Portugal	1960	3.01	2001	1.46
Republic of Korea	1960	5.98	1999	1.48
Romania	1960	2.33	2000	1.31
Russia	1960	2.56	2001	1.25
Slovakia	1960	3.07	2001	1.20
Spain	1960	2.86	2000	1.24
Sweden	1960	2.13	2001	1.57

Table continued on next page

Total Fertility Rates *(continued)*

	EARLIER DATE		LATER DATE	
COUNTRY	YEAR	TOTAL FERTILITY RATE	YEAR	TOTAL FERTILITY RATE
Switzerland	1960	2.44	2001	1.41
Ukraine	1960	2.23	1999	1.10
United Kingdom	1960	2.71	2000	1.65
United States	1960	3.65	2001	2.12

*Total fertility rate is the number of births that a woman would have in her life-time if, at each year of age, she experienced the birth rate occurring in the specified year.
Source: United Nations [5]

SNAPSHOT 6

Since 1970, the percentage of out-of-wedlock births has greatly increased among most developed nations.

* Among developed nations in 2000, Iceland had the highest percentage of out-of-wedlock births (65 percent), while Japan had the lowest (1 percent).

Percent of All Births That Were Out of Wedlock

	EARLIER DATE		LATER DATE	
COUNTRY	YEAR	PERCENT	YEAR	PERCENT
Australia	1970	8	1996	27
Belgium	1970	3	1995	17
Canada	1970	10	2000	38
Denmark	1970	11	1997	45
Finland	1970	6	2001	40
France	1970	7	2000	43
Germany	1970	9	2000	23
Greece	1970	1	1999	4
Iceland	1970	30	2000	65
Ireland	1970	3	2001	31
Italy	1970	2	2000	10
Japan	1970	1	1998	1
Netherlands	1970	2	2001	27
New Zealand	1970	13	1998	42
Norway	1970	7	2001	50
Portugal	1970	7	2001	24
Spain	1970	1	2000	18
Switzerland	1970	4	2001	11
United Kingdom	1970	8	2001	40
United States	1970	11	2002	34

Source: United Nations [6]

Snapshot 7

The United States has the highest teen birthrate among developed nations, while Japan has the lowest.

- In 2000, the United States teen birth rate was 48.7 births per thousand girls age 15-19, which was eleven times higher than that of Japan in 1997 (4.3).

Teen Birth Rates

Country	Births per 1,000 Women Age 15-19	Year
United States	48.7	2000
Russia Federation	44.7	1995
New Zealand	34.0	1996
United Kingdom	30.2	1997
Canada	24.5	1995
Portugal	21.3	1997
Australia	20.5	1995
Israel	16.7	1997
Ireland	16.1	1996
Austria	14.7	1997
Norway	12.8	1997
Greece	12.1	1997
Belgium	11.9	1992
Germany	9.7	1996
Finland	9.1	1997
Denmark	8.3	1996
France	7.9	1993
Sweden	7.8	1996
Spain	7.5	1996
Italy	6.8	1995
Switzerland	5.7	1996
Netherlands	5.6	1996
Japan	4.3	1997

Source: National Center for Health Statistics [7]

SNAPSHOT 8

In 2001, a higher percentage of American tenth graders had ever used marijuana, compared to their peers in Europe.

• In 2001, 41 percent of American tenth graders had ever used marijuana, compared to 10 percent of their Finnish peers.

Proportion of Tenth Graders Who Reported Ever Using Marijuana/Cannabis, 2001

COUNTRY	PERCENTAGE
United States	**41**
United Kingdom	35
France	35
Czech Republic	35
Ireland	32
The Netherlands	28
Slovenia	25
Italy	25
Denmark	24
Greenland	23
Russia (Moscow)	22
Ukraine	20
Slovak Republic	19
Latvia	17
Croatia	16
Iceland	15
Poland	14
Estonia	13
Norway	12
Lithuania	12
Bulgaria	12
Hungary	11
Finland	10
Greece	9
Sweden	8
Portugal	8
F.Y.R.O.M.	8
Malta	7
Faroe Islands	7
Cyprus	2
Romania	1

Source: European Survey Project on Alcohol and Drugs (ESPAD) [8]

SNAPSHOT 9

In 2001, illicit drug use (not including marijuana) among tenth graders was higher in the United States than in Europe.

- Compared to French tenth graders, nearly five times as many American tenth graders had ever used illicit drugs other than marijuana (24 percent v. 5 percent).

Proportion of Tenth Graders Who Reported Ever Using Illicit Drugs Other than Marijuana/Cannabis, 2001

COUNTRY	PERCENTAGE
United States	24
United Kingdom	12
Poland	11
Latvia	11
Russia (Moscow)	9
Romania	9
Lithuania	9
Ireland	9
Estonia	9
Czech Republic	9
Italy	8
Slovenia	7
Denmark	7
Portugal	6
Norway	6
Croatia	6
Slovak Republic	5
Iceland	5
Hungary	5
France	5
Bulgaria	5
Ukraine	4
Greenland	4
Greece	4
Sweden	3
Malta	3
Faroe Islands	3
F.Y.R.O.M.	3
Finland	2
Cyprus	2
The Netherlands	N/A

Source: European Survey Project on Alcohol and Drugs (ESPAD) [9]

NOTES

1   United Nations Population Division, "Partnership and Reproductive Behavior in Low-Fertility Countries," May 2003, Table 3.

2   Ibid and United Nations Population Division, *World Fertility Report 2003*, forthcoming.

3   United Nations Population Division, "Partnership and Reproductive Behavior in Low-Fertility Countries," Table 3 and United Nations Population Division, *World Fertility Report 2003*, forthcoming.

4   United Nations Population Division, "Partnership and Reproductive Behavior in Low-Fertility Countries," Table 7.

5   United Nations Population Division, "Partnership and Reproductive Behavior in Low-Fertility Countries," Table 22 and United Nations Population Division, *World Fertility Report 2003*, forthcoming.

6   United Nations Population Division, *World Fertility Report 2003*, forthcoming and United Nations Population Division, "Partnership and Reproductive Behavior in Low-Fertility Countries," Figure 10.

7   Stephanie J. Ventura, et al., *Births to Teenagers in the United States, 1940-2000*, National Vital Statistics Reports 49, National Center for Health Statistics, September 25, 2001, Table 7.

8   European Survey Project on Alcohol and Drugs (ESPAD), Press release available at *http://www.monitoringthefuture.org/pubs/espad_pr.pdf*.

9   Ibid.

FAMILY RESEARCH COUNCIL

Founded in 1983, the Family Research Council is a nonprofit research and educational organization dedicated to articulating and advancing a family-centered philosophy of public life. In addition to providing research and analysis for the legislative, executive, and judicial branches of the federal government, the Council seeks to inform the news media, the academic community, business leaders, and the public about family issues that affect the nation. Among its efforts to educate citizens for responsible engagement in public life is the Witherspoon Fellowship, a civic and cultural leadership program for college students.

The Family Research Council relies solely on the generosity of individuals, families, foundations, and businesses for financial support. The Internal Revenue Service recognizes FRC as a tax-exempt, 501(c)(3) charitable organization. Donations are therefore tax-deductible in accordance with Section 170 of the Internal Revenue Code.

Located at 801 G Street, N.W., Washington, D.C., the headquarters of the Family Research Council provides its staff with strategic access to government decision-making centers, national media offices, and information sources. Owned by Faith Family Freedom, L.L.C., the six-story building was completed in 1996 through the generosity of the Edgar Prince and the Richard DeVos families of western Michigan. Visitors are welcome during normal business hours. Please call (202) 393-2100 in advance to ensure a pleasant and productive visit.